FRANCIS AND JESUS

Francis and Jesus

MURRAY BODO

Franciscan
MEDIA
Cincinnati, Ohio

Excerpts from Marion A. Habig, O.F.M., *St. Francis of Assisi: writings and early biographies: English omnibus of the sources for the life of St. Francis* (Cincinnati: St. Anthony Messenger Press, 2008) are used by permission. All rights reserved.

Scripture passages have been taken from *New Revised Standard Version Bible,* copyright ©1989 by the Division of Christian Education of the National Council of the Churches of Christ in the U.S.A., and used by permission. All rights reserved.

Cover and book design by Mark Sullivan
Cover image:
Saint Francis receiving the Stigmata, detail of Saint Francis, c.1297-99 (fresco)
by Giotto di Bondone (c.1266-1337)
San Francesco, Upper Church, Assisi, Italy
© bridgemanart.com

LIBRARY OF CONGRESS CATALOGING-IN-PUBLICATION DATA
Bodo, Murray.
Francis and Jesus / Murray Bodo.
p. cm.
ISBN 978-0-86716-995-9 (alk. paper)
1. Francis, of Assisi, Saint, 1182-1226. 2. Christian saints—Italy—Assisi—Biography. I. Title.
BX4700.F6B5554 2012
271'.302—dc23
[B]
2012036802

ISBN 978-0-86716-995-9
Copyright ©2012, Murray Bodo. All rights reserved.

Published by Franciscan Media
28 W. Liberty St.
Cincinnati, OH 45202
www.FranciscanMedia.org

Printed in the United States of America.
Printed on acid-free paper.

13 14 15 16 17 5 4 3 2 1

Joy fall to thee, father Francis,
Drawn to the Life that died,
With the gnarls of the nails in thee, niche of the lance, his
Lovescape crucified
And seal of his seraph-arrival!

—Gerard Manley Hopkins,
"The Wreck of the Deutschland"

In memory of my mother
Polly Bonan Bodo, 1913–1989

Full many a flower is born to blush unseen
And waste its sweetness on the desert air.
—Thomas Gray,
"Elegy Written in a Country Churchyard," 1751

CONTENTS

FOREWORD

"Do you think that I have come to bring peace to the earth? No, I tell you, but rather division!"

—Luke 12:51

I offer this probably disappointing, or perhaps surprising line from Jesus to lead you into a book that will be anything but disappointing and very happily surprising. Jesus said it to his disciples after they began to experience their own disappointments and failures, and he seemed to be telling them *not* to be surprised and not even to be disappointed. It was and will always be the necessary pattern.

Great Truth divides before it unites, separates before it reconciles; anything great creates division before it brings peace. It splits the heart and mind open before it later makes them whole. And in the meantime we all take sides. This prediction and warning of Jesus has surely been true for over two thousand years. He is either hated or loved, worshiped or dismissed by every century and every group—but in very different ways and for different reasons. And further, some seem to love him for the wrong reasons—to merely save themselves. While others reject him for the right reasons—they know *he is asking for everything* and they are not ready to give everything.

Now and again, certain people appear who make the division very clear—and then leap in themselves to overcome it—they fill the tragic gaps of hearts and history with the vitality of their own lives and the abundance of the one Spirit. Some are ready to give *the everything* that Divine Encounter makes possible. Such a person was Francis of Assisi. He endured and taught with his life the splitting open and then the more lovely reuniting. It is only this second union, or better re-union, that is our full goal. The peace of the Holy Spirit is not just naive contentment, but precisely, conflict overcome. It is always division undone.

You are about to be led on a wonderful journey with both Jesus and Francis, by a Franciscan brother of mine and a fellow New Mexican, Fr. Murray Bodo, who has earned the right to speak about both of them. He knows that Jesus is always too much for us, so we need people to lead the way, to open the lens, to show us that Great Truth must and will always be lived in little and unique ways.

It is the only way Greatness can be packaged and presented, and so the hallmarks of the man from Assisi rightly became humility, poverty, and littleness. And rejoicing in the same! Francis was happy to be a small stage for the Big Act that is always taking place, which is the eternal and flowing life of God. He, as Jesus himself, made that One Life beautiful and believable in space and time.

Francis of Assisi seemed to love and follow Jesus for the utterly right reasons. Like all true lovers, he wanted only to seek the beloved, serve the beloved, and become one with the beloved. There was no other goal or desire in his life, and so it purified everything, down to every motivation and daily activity.

As Soren Kierkegaard so beautifully put it, "purity of heart is to will one thing." No wonder Jesus said that the pure of heart would see God (see Matthew 5:8). They alone keep their eyes in one constant and consistent direction, and thus overcome the divisions that are created by our divided hearts and our divided loyalties. Such people are like giant spotlights that open and illuminate the path for the rest of us.

In this lovely book, we can stand and walk in the light of perhaps two of the greatest spotlights the world has ever received, Jesus and Francis; and you will see that they create one bright beam of light, more than enough light to overcome any darkness (see John 1:5). As William Blake put it, "We are put on earth a little space, that we may learn to bear the beams of love."

I thank Murray Bodo for making those beams accessible and illuminating for so many of us. There is no division here, but only the final and full *peace* that Jesus came to bring. Now there is no time to take sides but only the recognition of an *abyss* and *ground* so great and so beautiful that we can only admit that we are all in free fall.

—*Fr. Richard Rohr,* o.f.m.
Center for Action
and Contemplation
Albuquerque, New Mexico

ACKNOWLEDGMENTS

Once many moons ago in Assisi, Fr. Damien Isabell, O.F.M., the founder of Franciscan Study Pilgrimages said to me, "If you want a thumbnail description of Francis and his first companions, I would say they were poor, itinerant, preaching brothers of penance." That insight rang true to me and stuck with me over the years and has now made its way into the Introduction and spirit of this book. I am grateful to Fr. Damien for this and many other insights he shared with me when we worked together on Franciscan Study Pilgrimages.

I gratefully acknowledge the scholarship of Fr. Theophile Desbonnets, O.F.M., whose book, *Assise sur le pas de saint Francois*, was invaluable in framing the chronology.

I also want to thank my confrere, Fr. Richard Rohr, for his brilliant foreword; my editors Mark Lombard and Kathleen Carroll, and my reader, Judith Emery, for their careful reading and editing of the text, their questions and suggestions, and for their encouragement, which enabled me to continue working on this book.

INTRODUCTION

The brothers who lived with him knew how his daily and continuous talk was of Jesus and how sweet and tender his conversation was, how kind and filled with love his talk with them. His mouth spoke out of the abundance of his heart, and the fountain of enlightened love that filled his whole being bubbled forth outwardly. Indeed, he was always occupied with Jesus; Jesus he bore in his heart, Jesus in his mouth, Jesus in his ears, Jesus in his eyes, Jesus in his hands, Jesus in the rest of his members....

And because he bore and preserved Christ Jesus and him crucified in his heart with a wonderful love, he was marked in a most glorious way above all others with the seal of him whom in a rapture of mind he contemplated sitting in inexpressible and incomprehensible glory at the right hand of the Father....

—Thomas of Celano, *First Life of St. Francis*

The ultimate disciple. The poor, itinerant, preaching brother of penance. He who suffered in the wilderness with Christ, he who was misunderstood, betrayed by some of his own brothers, and who loved Christ so much that he became the Lovescape of Christ. This is St. Francis of Assisi.

The great poet, Gerard Manley Hopkins, invented the word "Lovescape" to encapsulate how he saw St. Francis's relationship with Jesus Christ. Francis was Christ's "Lovescape crucified and seal of his seraph-arrival." He is speaking of Francis on the mountain of La Verna, where he received the sacred stigmata of Christ that sealed him as a visible image of the Crucified Christ, Christ's "Lovescape."

On La Verna St. Francis's transformation into Christ was made visible in his body through the visitation of a seraph-angel whose six wings surrounded the body of the Risen Crucified Christ. Francis had become the very personification of Christ's words, "You will know that I am in my Father, and you in me, and I in you" (John 14:20). When you look at St. Francis, you see the Crucified Christ whose presence within Francis was so real and so intense that the very wounds of Christ Crucified broke forth in his body, revealing to the whole world that here, indeed, was the ultimate disciple of Christ, who not only bore in his body the wounds of Christ, but whose heart was filled with the love that moved Christ to suffer for love of us. As St. Francis himself articulates so beautifully in one of the prayers attributed to him, "May the fiery and honey-sweet power of your love, O Lord, wean me from all things under heaven, so that I may die for love of your love, who deigned to die for love of my love."[1]

Where, then, did this transformation begin and how did it come about? It all began with two transforming events in the young Francis Bernardone's life: the embrace of a leper and his attendance at Mass on what was then the Feast of St. Matthias, February 24, 1208. Both events represent the radical poverty of St. Francis and how Gospel poverty defined who he was.

This radical poverty, in the words of the medieval Franciscan poet Jacopone da Todi, is this:

> Poverty is to have nothing
> And to desire nothing
> And to possess everything
> In a spirit of freedom.[2]

It seems from these lines that to have nothing and desire nothing is what Franciscan poverty is all about, but it is the last line, "in a spirit of freedom," that is the essence. It was not letting go of things that made St. Francis Christ's Lovescape, but letting go of his ego. His had been a grand ambition: He wanted, a merchant's son though he was, to become a knight, to ascend through military prowess to the ranks of the nobility. He desired to be somebody, to be influential, to matter. But in his first foray into war, he was captured in a decisive battle between Assisi and the neighboring hill town of Perugia and spent a year in a Perugian prison. It is said that he tried to cheer his fellow soldiers, but his health began to decline; and when he returned to Assisi a year later, he was a broken man who had to spend another year recuperating.

When he finally was able to venture outdoors again, nothing seemed the same; the glow of nature no longer shone for him. Was he in a state of post-traumatic shock? Was he simply depressed? Whatever the case, the things that before had stimulated and excited him—the revels, the beauties of nature, singing and dancing—no longer lifted his spirit, until one day when he heard about another call to arms, this time to join the papal forces in Apulia, south of Rome, under the command of the celebrated Walter of Brienne.

Francis was now awakened from his torpor and once again set forth with other Assisi cavaliers to join the papal armies. But after only one day on the road he had a dream in the nearby city of Spoleto in which a voice asked him,

"Francis, who is it better to serve, the Lord or the servant?"

"Why, the Lord, of course."

"Then why are you serving the servant?"

Then, in a moment of insight, of epiphany, Francis realized that he had it all wrong, and he returned to Assisi, not knowing what he was supposed to do, or even what he was searching for. He began to visit abandoned churches and caves where he prayed incessantly for enlightenment.

Then one day when he was riding his horse on the road below Assisi, he saw a leper on the road and was moved to get down off his high horse, as it were—a huge gesture for the ambitious young man— and not only place coins in the leper's outstretched hand, but on an extraordinary impulse, he actually embraced the leper, realizing as he did so, that he was embracing *the* Lord, Jesus Christ, who is also the Servant. In embracing this servant, he was paradoxically embracing the Lord. He had relinquished the dominance of his ego. He was no longer paralyzed. He was free.

In overcoming himself and embracing the leper, Francis found true Gospel poverty; he found a poverty that was a new kind of riches. Now he had only to rid himself of whatever else was keeping him from this hidden treasure he had found. He discovered what that was in the small chapel of St. Mary of the Angels, hidden among the woods and marshes of the plain where the lepers lived.

It was February 24, 1208, and Francis was attending Mass; at the reading of the Gospel, he heard the Gospel passage that changed his life. It not only completed his vision of poverty, but it also gave him the lifestyle he was to embrace. And this is how it was, as his first biographer, Thomas of Celano, narrates it:

> But when on a certain day the Gospel was read in that church, how the Lord sent his disciples out to preach, the holy man of God, assisting there, understood somewhat the words of the Gospel; and after Mass he humbly asked the priest to explain the Gospel to him more fully. When the priest had set forth in order all these things, the holy Francis, hearing that Christ's disciples should not possess gold or silver or money; nor carry along the way scrip, or wallet, or bread, or a staff; that they should not have shoes, or two tunics; but that they should preach the kingdom of God and penance, he immediately cried out exultingly: "This is what I wish, this is what I seek, this is what I long to do with all my heart."[3]

And that is what Francis did; he became what Jesus asked his disciples to become: a poor, itinerant, preaching brother of penance. He took to the road, he had no fixed abode, and he was brother to everyone he met along the way and to all of creation. And he became a brother in another way he never anticipated. Other men joined him, and they became a brotherhood who embraced lepers and lived out the Gospel passage, the form of life given to them in the Gospel for the Mass of St. Matthias. St. Francis relates the coming of the brothers in these words:

> And after the Lord gave me some brothers, no one showed me what do; but the Most High revealed to me that I was

to live after the manner of the Holy Gospel. And I had it written down in brief, simple words and the Lord Pope confirmed it for me. And those who came to receive this life gave everything to the poor, and they were happy with one tunic patched inside and out, and with a cord and breeches. And we had no desire for anything else.[4]

And Francis himself began to fall deeper and deeper in love with the Christ he met in the leper and in all those other servants who were really Christ: the poor, the marginal, those rejected by society, the weak, the infirm, the powerless. For, in loving Christ, Francis realized that the servant is the Lord, and the Lord is the servant. More importantly, he realized that the penance he was to preach, and his brothers were to preach, is the penance of conversion, of letting go of one's ego and surrendering to a love which to others seems madness, but to the true lover is sanity.

True, even to a deeply committed disciple like St. Francis, the embrace of Christ can feel at times like annihilation, like death itself, because in fact one is dying to something. One is dying to a false self that tries to be God, that tries to always be in control. But that dying is really life, the new life Jesus promised to those who relinquish their own willfulness as he did when he said in the Garden of Gethsemane, "My Father, if it is possible, may this cup be taken from me. Yet not as I will but as you will." That surrendering of his own will to the Father's will was the beginning of Christ's Resurrection and our resurrection, for by accepting the cup the Father offers us, we accept death, but a death that is life-giving.

But lest all this death and dying and annihilation begin to sound off-putting or unnecessarily negative, it is important to keep in mind that it is love that is the true disciple's motivation for what at times may seem a negative way to live one's life. For such a life is only *seemingly* negative; in fact, it brings great joy, for the freedom to love the Beloved is the fruit of this penance, this conversion from a selfish, ego-centric life to a Christo-centric vision and way of living. Only in letting go of the primacy of the ego does the primacy of Christ reign in one's life. And once that happens then everything that exists is yours. It is yours because you are not trying to possess it, to appropriate it to yourself, but to love it as Christ loved it and continues to love it through and in you. This is the freedom that Jacopone da Todi was talking about in the lines that began this meditation:

> and to possess everything
> in a spirit of freedom.

This was the freedom that prompted St. Francis's song of joy, "The Canticle of the Creatures," which he sang two years before he died, even though he lay emaciated, blind, seriously ill, and hemorrhaging with the wounds of Christ. Unable to take the pain and darkness any longer, he cried aloud to God, and God spoke to him words of promise and love:

> One night, as he was thinking of all the tribulations he was enduring, he felt sorry for himself and said interiorly: "Lord, help me in my infirmities so that I may have the strength to bear them patiently!" And suddenly he heard a voice in spirit: "Tell me, Brother: if, in compensation for your

sufferings and tribulations you were given an immense and precious treasure: the whole mass of the earth changed into pure gold, pebbles into precious stones, and the water of the rivers into perfume, would you not regard the waters and pebbles as nothing compared to such a treasure? Would you not rejoice?" Blessed Francis answered: "Lord, it would be a very great, a very precious, and inestimable treasure beyond all that one can love and desire!" "Well, brother, the voice said, "be glad and joyful in the midst of your infirmities and tribulations: as of now, live in peace as if you were already sharing my kingdom."[5]

The following pages tell the story of how St. Francis came to share God's kingdom even while he was still on earth, and how he came to possess everything he thought he had given away. It is the story of what it means to be a true disciple of Jesus, the story of how true discipleship is born of a love for Jesus that transforms the disciple into the Christ in whose footsteps the true disciple walks. Few have expressed this truth more beautifully than Gerard Manley Hopkins in these lines from his exquisite Petrarchan sonnet, "As Kingfishers Catch Fire":

> Each mortal thing does one thing and the same:
> Deals out that being indoors each one dwells;
> Selves—goes itself; *myself* it speaks and spells,
> Crying *What I do is me: for that I came.*
> I say more: the just man justices;
> Keeps grace: that keeps all his goings graces;
> Acts in God's eye what in God's eye he is—

Christ—for Christ plays in ten thousand places,
Lovely in limbs, and lovely in eyes not his
To the Father through the features of men's faces.[6]

Such a face was the face of St. Francis of Assisi; such a face is that of everyone who walks in the footsteps of Jesus Christ. Here then is the story of St. Francis's own transformation into the Christ he loved above everything and everyone, the Christ whose "Lovescape" he became.

THE YEAR OF OUR LORD 1209

A New Life

He loved Rome. Not the way he loved the Umbrian Valley, or the way some seemed to love Rome for its teeming life, or the grandeur of the Basilica of St. John Lateran, or the whimsical flow of visitors and pilgrims, but for the way the sun lit the buildings from the Gianiculum Hill and the distant hum of history in its streets and the color and pageantry of its processions and liturgies. But most of all he loved Rome for the Basilica of St. Peter, the Prince of the Apostles, who pleased the Lord Jesus, who once asked Simon Peter, "Who do you say that I am?" And he answered, "You are the Messiah, the Son of the living God" (Matthew 16:16). And Jesus said, "Blessed are you, Simon son of Jonah! For flesh and blood has not revealed this to you, but my Father in heaven. And I tell you, you are Peter, and on this rock I will build my church" (Matthew 16:17–18).

Francis loved the part about flesh and blood not revealing this, but "my Father in heaven." He was moved to tears, remembering his own experience, what it was that had brought him and his brothers to Rome, to the feet of the successor of St. Peter, Pope Innocent III, to ask his approval of the brothers' way of life. Francis's own experience came, as St. Peter's response had come, from his Father in heaven.

. . . .

He had returned from a year's imprisonment in Perugia as a prisoner of war only a few months before and was weak and troubled in spirit. He had lain abed unable to rise, and only the desire to return to the field of battle kept him going. He had to get well; he had to prove himself worthy of Knighthood. He had to feel the sword of a great lord on his shoulder and hear the word, "Sir," before his name, or he would die of shame. He had to be a worthy warrior.

And so he persevered: through the fevers, the despondency, the feeling of worthlessness, the darkened room, his mother's anxiety, his father's disappointment. Most of all, he persevered through the sense of time wasted, time passing without his life making any difference. No battles won, no orphans and widows protected, no dragons slain. The Round Table had become a rectangle, a bed on which he tossed and turned and feared he would lose sight of the Quest, the call to serve the good pleasure of a lord, or maybe even a King.

. . . .

A gull screamed where he stood lost in memory on the bank of the darkening Tiber, the brothers around him thinking him lost in prayer. Or was this really prayer, after all, this reverie that led him always to fall on his knees in thanksgiving for the Lord and King whom his longing for knighthood had led him to, this Lord of all, who filled him still with awe and gratitude and love which no earthly lord could possibly have engendered in his heart? This Lord Jesus, this Lord of heaven and earth.

He turned to his brothers and seeing them, fell to his knees in gratitude for what had just taken place in God's mercy and love. The Lord Pope Innocent III had approved a way of life that Jesus himself had given them. May his name be praised forever.

But something further, a grace unanticipated had been given to him as he prayed throughout the night after Pope Innocent had heard his request and told him to go and pray that God would show the Pope what God wanted him to do. That very night Pope Innocent and Francis had both dreamed the dream that revealed the Lord's will that made of these brothers standing on the Tiber's bank more than a band of men united in their love of Christ and his Gospel. Now they were being sent forth to preach and witness in the power of the Holy Spirit given them by Holy Mother Church. And Francis himself had become a mother like mother Church.

Francis looked into the faces of his sons eagerly waiting for God's word given to him in his contemplation of the Tiber. He loved them all: Bernard of Quintavalle, Peter Catanii, Sylvester, Giles, Sabbatino, Morico, John of Capella, Philip, Barbaro, Bernard of Viridente, Angelo Tancredi.

"Brothers, do you know what has happened to us because of the gift of dreams? You heard the Lord Pope's dream and the dream I recounted to the Pope. His Holiness told us how he saw the Basilica of St. John Lateran falling, and how a poor beggar had rushed forward to support the falling church with his shoulder. Each of you, my brothers, is that poor beggar. No sword is placed upon your shoulders like a man being knighted, but the pillars of the church itself rest on your shoulders. And that is what we are now sent to do. We are the shoulders supporting the church, lest it fall.

"And what of my dream of how a king passing through the desert saw a poor woman there and fell in love with her? Of how he had many sons by her who, the king said, were always welcome at his court where he would clothe and feed them. You are those sons, my dear brothers, and Christ is your Father, the King of heaven and earth. And I, unworthy though I am, in God's unfathomable plan, am your mother, the poor woman of the desert, who will love each of you forever, hoping as I do so that you in turn will love one another as a mother loves the child of her flesh.

"This is what we are sent to be: shoulders for the church and sons of the Great King and mothers to one another and all those whom we give birth to through Christ's intimate love for us, and we for him.

"So let us now follow the Tiber upstream to our beloved Umbria, being along the way what we have been sent to be."

Francis felt the road beneath his bare feet. He looked at the Tiber and reflected that they were walking against the flow of the water, back to their origins in the Umbrian Valley. To Assisi, Spoleto, San Damiano, the Porziuncola. To the lepers among whom he and the brothers would again embrace Christ.

. . . .

He thought of his father and mother, of his childhood home, and of the dreams and voices that changed everything forever.

How carefree he'd been as a boy, how proud to be the son of the great cloth merchant Pietro Bernardone. How sweet and kind a mother was Lady Pica. How much pain he'd caused his parents when he renounced his father's patrimony and declared he would never again say, "My father Pietro Bernardone," but "Our Father who art in heaven." How grandiose that sounded now. Yet, that is the way of the following of Christ.

. . . .

The brothers' singing shook him from his reverie and he joined them in singing the "Salve Regina," that lovely hymn to Mary he'd learned as a boy at his mother's knee.

Hail, holy Queen, mother of mercy,
hail, our life, our sweetness, and our hope.
To you do we cry,
poor banished children of Eve.
To you do we send up our sighs,
mourning and weeping in this valley of tears.
Turn then, most gracious advocate,
your eyes of mercy toward us,
and after this, our exile,
show to us the blessed fruit of your womb, Jesus.
O clement, O loving,
O sweet Virgin Mary.

But even as he sang, Francis could not keep his mind from wandering.

. . . .

He was back in Assisi, having returned weakened and ill from
that year's imprisonment in Perugia, his dream of knighthood
dashed to the ground at Ponte San Giovanni, where the Assisi
forces were defeated and Francis was taken prisoner, an experience that profoundly changed him and prepared him for the
dreams God was to send him.

Prison. The damp walls, the stench of urine and feces and
vomit, the moaning of the wounded, the panic that he could
not escape, that he could be there for years. And then there
was the darkness. How he hated the dark, he who had loved
to swing open the shutters of his home and let in the morning
sunlight rising over Mount Subasio. Now there was only this
clammy darkness and despair and the stench of his own beautiful clothes, the finery beneath his armor that he had been so
proud of. It became so bad that he had to take off his clothes
altogether and fling them into a corner and sit or stand or lie
down in his breeches, they, too, becoming fetid as the days and
weeks and months of darkness dragged on, his only light being
the good cheer he tried to impart to his fellow soldiers as he
sought to emulate the courage and cheerfulness he imagined
his knight heroes always displayed.

And when, after a year, he finally returned to Assisi, he lay
in bed for over a year in what seemed now a coma of misery,
his mother's anxious ministrations attending to his every need.
Much of the time his father was away, attending to his affairs
and properties in the country or on cloth-buying trips to
the Champagne in France. And when he returned, he, too,

seemed nervous, hiding his anxiety by telling Francis stories of
the journey and of the court of Marie de Champagne and her
troubadour, Chretien de Troyes, whose stories of Arthur and
the Knights of the Round Table had so enchanted him before.
Now they sounded hollow and far from the reach of his weak
arms and heart and imagination.

How spiritually dark were those months in bed before he
could finally rise and go to the window and look out onto the
noisy street below, or raise his eyes to the sky and walk through
the city gates and down into the countryside where his father's
fields lay open to the sky.

When it finally happened that he could go outside into the
country, he stood in disbelief that the songs of the birds and the
paths that wound down from the city between the olive groves
gave him no joy. He turned and looked up at Mount Subasio
towering above, and even the mountain's challenge no longer
thrilled him.

Something terrible had happened to him. Or so it seemed
then when he thought that was the end of it all, that he would
remain in this melancholic state forever. But, as he eventually understood, what was really coming to pass was God's slow
working within him. He was being prepared for that reversal
which is in fact a turning toward. Toward what, though? Was it
not a turning toward what had been there all along: the Spirit
of God within him preparing him for the birth of Jesus Christ
in his life, the sweet birth of his Savior?

He did not know then what he learned later: God works
in silence, God works in a darkness in which we think he

has abandoned us, that he is no longer there. Back then he thought only of his misery and discouragement which, he was convinced, came from not being able to continue the pursuit of knighthood. And so, as soon as he was well, he set off from Assisi again in response to the call of the Lord Pope Innocent to join the papal forces in Apulia under the command of the great Walter of Brienne, a commander who could knight Francis if he proved worthy in battle. He set off again because of a dream he had in which he saw the great hall of a castle on whose walls hung many shields that a voice assured him were those of Francis and his knights. What other proof had he needed that the cause of his melancholy was the unfulfilled call to knighthood?

And so he set off with other Assisi soldiers and knights to Apulia, stopping the first night in Spoleto. O, how fateful was that night on which he dreamed the dream of the castle hall once more! Here they were again, the shields of Francis and his knights. And then, the fateful voice:

"Francis, who is it better to serve, the lord or the servant?"

"Why, the lord, of course."

"Then why are you serving the servant? Go now, and return to Assisi where it will be shown you what you are to do."

How bitter those words tasted when he woke with the words still echoing in his ears and he knowing somehow that the words were real, more than a dream, that they came from an Angel, or could it be, from God Himself?

And that is how it happened that he deserted his fellow soldiers in Spoleto and returned, a despondent, seeming coward, to Assisi and to his disappointed, disbelieving father, his confused and anxious mother.

He was ashamed to face anyone, including his poor parents. And so he spent his days in bed or roaming aimlessly the paths below the city, visiting abandoned churches, or climbing the side of Mount Subasio looking for caves to hide in and listen for the voice that would enlighten his darkness and show him what he was supposed to do.

He walked and waited, prayed and wept and thought he would go mad. Why had he dreamed the two dreams? Were they real or not real? From God, or from his sick and twisted mind deceiving him? Was the dream at Spoleto caused only by his fear of going back to war and being captured again? But were not dreams from God, as the priests taught? And was not the Holy Word of God itself filled with dreams? And on and on, thus.

His mother worried for him, his father, angry and disappointed, left more often, it seemed, to attend to matters away from Assisi, and Francis felt worse by the day—until one day when he was praying, as he often did, in the rundown roadside chapel of San Damiano below Assisi's walls. Yes, he had begun to pray! More accurately, he had begun to listen prayerfully.

He was kneeling before the crucifix that hung above the small altar when suddenly it seemed that Christ's eyes looked upon him…and he heard the voice.

"Francis, go and repair my house which, as you see, is falling into ruin."

He waited, breathless. Waited and listened and trembled. But the eyes of the crucified Christ remained fixed in space as before. The chapel was still. There was no voice. No sound but the sound of the wind soughing in the olive trees outside.

But he had heard the promised voice, and it was the same voice he'd heard at Spoleto. And it had come from his Crucified Savior. Jesus had shown him what to do. Jesus.

He could not remember how long he'd knelt there, his soul flooded with gratitude and with overwhelming love for Jesus. So this was his Lord. No earthly king or lord, but the Lord Jesus Christ, King of heaven and earth. And his Lord was asking of him the simplest of tasks that felt like the most sublime mission, the heavenly "Arthur" sending him forth from this table, this poor small altar, to repair this very chapel. How like something King Arthur would do to test a proud knight!

He rose to his feet, kissed the feet of the crucifix and ran full speed into the city, stunning those who knew him and who had seen till now this melancholy young man shuffling, head down, in and out of the city gates.

He burst into his father's shop—his father mercifully was once again away on a cloth-buying trip—and laying hold of a bolt of fine cloth, he ran from the shop into the stable where he mounted one of his father's horses.

Horse and rider then clattered over the cobblestones to the city gates and galloped toward the city of Foligno where Francis knew he could sell the cloth and the horse.

. . . .

He saw now, as he walked along silently with the brothers, that selling the cloth and horse contained everything that he and the brothers were to be: horseless, clothesless servants of the Great King. They would walk barefoot, they would give away their finery and clothe their nakedness with the poor vesture of Jesus.

. . . .

He sold the cloth and horse almost immediately, and taking the money, walked, skipped rather, back to San Damiano where he offered the money to the astonished impoverished priest who lived there, eagerly telling him that the money was for the repair of San Damiano.

But the priest refused the money.

"Francis, are you mad? I know your father; you know your father. When he returns, he will come after both of us for this money. And he will punish me for catering to this whim of yours."

"But, father, Christ told me to do this."

"Oh, did he? Well, he told me just the opposite, namely, that this money belongs to your father and must be returned to him. Now run along and don't come back and disturb my peace with your games, Francesco di Bernardone."

But he was undaunted. He threw the money onto the chapel's window sill and ran toward the city, calling back to the frightened priest, "Then I will beg stones and rebuild the church myself."

"Sure you will, you pampered, soft son of Bernardone!"

But that is what Francis did, to the astonishment of the priest of San Damiano.

He had feared his father's return. What would he say when he found his son missing, when he heard the rumors of his mad son, when he saw the missing bolt of cloth and the missing horse?

The reality matched his anticipation. His father was furious, not especially with the loss of his possessions because, after all, his good-hearted son had always been prodigal with his father's goods, but out of shame, hearing that Francis had gone mad and was begging stones to work on restoring the chapel of San Damiano. Francis knew that his father could personally pay for the restoration of the chapel, and he would probably have entertained the idea had Francis pressed hard enough, but this new direction Francis was taking—that was what his father could not tolerate. Was it not enough that Francis had come home from the war in Apulia, having traveled only a day's journey? Was it not enough that he had been moping about the countryside, not working in the shop; or when he did, doing so with no enthusiasm—so unlike his former joy in talking to buyers, in showing them the beautiful cloth, in listening to and sharing in the gossip of the town? And now this!

How disappointed and angry Pietro had been! And the more he thought about what Francis was doing, the angrier he became until his rage moved him to throw Francis into the small prison within the family home and lock him in. Another darkness, less terrifying than the prison in Perugia, but darkness all the same, a darkness more inner than outer, a darkness of confusion about how he was going to sort out mother and father, Jesus and his Father.

Shortly afterward Pietro went on another trip to buy cloth which made Francis wonder now if his father hadn't needed to get away from the townspeople's mockery of his son.

And so he lay in the family prison ministered to again by his mother who brought him food and fresh clothes, who took his chamber pot to be emptied and who breaking his chains, released him as soon as his father was safely far enough from Assisi.

His poor mother! He remembered now the look of amazement on her face when he kissed her and told her that he was leaving to live with the poor priest of San Damiano while he continued to work on the church. He tried to explain, and his mother tried hard to hear him, to understand; but he knew, even as he spoke tenderly to her, that she was unable to really understand what he was doing, though she believed that he had somehow heard God's voice. But how could God ask such a thing of her, to let her dear son leave home before it was time, before he had his father's blessing?

She could only stammer that she loved him and wished he could at least live at home while he worked on the church. And he could only stammer that he could not, that God was calling him to a place he himself did not fully understand. He only knew that he had to go. And so they parted tearfully, though as soon as Francis began to walk away from the city, his heart lifted, and in his joy and enthusiasm he forgot the look on his mother's face, so compelled was he by this new work, this new life. It pained him now to remember her face and realize that he actually wanted to leave her, that he wanted to have a life without her. How could he have felt that way toward someone whose love was so unselfish, so good? Even now he could not understand; he could only remember Christ's words—he had to do what was his to do: "Repair my house, which, as you see, is falling into ruins."

And so it happened that he hid away in a place the priest of San Damiano provided for him, a dark closet that somehow didn't seem dark, a darkness he was getting used to, a darkness that was almost light.

And the priest now seemed more enthused by seeing the church slowly being repaired than he was afraid of Bernardone who would soon return again to Assisi.

And Francis continued to pray and work and beg stones and now even to beg food, breaking his mother's heart who longed to give him any food he wanted, who longed to sit with him at table. And the people of Assisi? They mocked him mostly, though some seemed to pity him and even gave him a stone from time to time, this poor demented son of rich Pietro Bernardone. His brother Angelo would mock him every time he saw him, as did some of his former friends and companions who before used to hang on his every word and even more firmly hang on to his purse strings. All of which filled him with joy instead of the bitterness the last thought seemed to suggest: namely, that they loved him for his money. He felt no bitterness. He simply kept his mind's eye fixed on the crucifix of San Damiano, his ear attuned to the quest that the great King of the

Universe had given him.

And then came the paternal reckoning. His father returned, and this time he became so enraged with his wife that he came close to striking Lady Pica. Instead he jumped onto one of the horses and raced down to San Damiano. Bellowing Francis's name, he demanded that Francis return all his goods and the sooner the better. Then, losing all control, he jumped from his horse and screamed at his son, demanding further that Francis appear before the mayor of Assisi for the redress of the injustice he had done to his father.

How surprised his father was and how even more surprised was Francis that he had refused. He stood up to his father—the dark closet had become light. He stood before his father and said he would not go before the civil magistrate because he was now under the jurisdiction of the bishop.

His father lifted his arm as if to strike him, but seeing the determination in his son's eyes, or remembering he was his son, or simply out of a fear of the mad rage that would have killed his son had he started to strike him, he dropped his arm instead and said with a cold, almost eerie calm, "Fine, then I will see you in the Bishop's court, that useless pawn of the Pope." And he turned and mounted his horse and rode pell-mell into the city.

How could his father have known that Francis had been discussing God's words to him with Bishop Guido, who had been sympathetic, interested. Was it only because now the Bishop would have a wedge into the heart of Pietro Bernardone, or because he was getting a free repair of San Damiano? Or did he, as Francis believed, see something Divine in all this madness? Did Bishop Guido want to believe that Francis was being called by God to serve the Church? Whatever the reason, he told Francis that in this matter between him and his father, the Bishop himself would be the arbiter since Francis was in the process of leaving the world to enter the Church.

And so it happened.

He had prayed all night, prayed and struggled to overcome fear as he knelt before the great King, who hung upon the cross of San Damiano, Christ's open eyes staring into Francis's soul. He was about to renounce his father Pietro, leave his mother Lady Pica, and begin a quest that only this King knew the end of. Only this Lord Jesus Christ knew what was to happen this morning in the Bishop's courtyard.

He asked the priest of San Damiano for his blessing. "Go, Francis, child of God, and be brave. Your good heart will triumph in Him who gives you comfort and strength. In the name of the Father, and of the Son, and of the Holy Spirit. Amen."

With the money he'd thrown onto the windowsill and only the clothes he wore, which was all he had in his possession, Francis walked the longest and the shortest walk of his life: the short walk from San Damiano to the Bishop's palace next to the Church of St. Mary Major and the longer walk into his new life as yet to be revealed.

People for once were not mocking him as he walked along, head held high, a smile on his face. They were somber. They knew what was going to happen. The rumors had been circulating for days. They stepped aside when he passed.

His heart pounded as he finally stepped into the courtyard and saw so many of the townspeople and the Bishop seated on his throne, his father Pietro at the Bishop's side, and his poor mother standing behind, a look of unabashed agony on her face.

He almost faltered, but seeing that he just might, he did what would become a pattern from then on. He did something outrageous that dispelled all fear. He began to undress. He kept undressing, down to his underpants. And then in what must have seemed a mad gesture that liberated his whole being, he took off even his underpants and stood there naked; and holding the clothes and the money bag before him, he walked to his father and placed them all at his feet, saying calmly but deliberately to his father, the Bishop, and all those present, "Up till now I have called Pietro Bernardone my father. From now on I will no longer say, my father Pietro Bernardone, but Our Father who art in heaven."

The shock and shame on his father's face and the flushed face of his mother, her eyes downcast, wrenched his heart, but he did not flinch. And no one moved—until Bishop Guido, in a dramatic fatherly gesture, draped his cope around Francis and took him inside where he clothed him in a peasant's garb before leading him outside again. And still there was silence. No further words were needed.

Then Francis calmly walked out of the courtyard wondering where in the world he was going. His steps were someone other's. He was being led. He walked toward Gubbio. There, at least, he could get away and talk with his friend, Federico Spadalungo. Why there? He didn't know. It was simply somewhere to go.

He didn't look back. He didn't know what the Bishop and his father and his mother did next. He couldn't hear the assembled crowd. He walked away, out the city gates toward Gubbio. He walked, a lone peasant on the road.

Still trembling from the event that had just taken place in the Bishop's courtyard, Francis suddenly broke into a run. He began to feel joy as the peasant's garb he wore flapped in the wind, and his feet jumped lightly over the stones of the steep descent from Assisi toward the road that led to Gubbio.

Before the Bishop led him out into the courtyard, the Bishop had chalked a cross on the old tunic that had once belonged to one of Bishop Guido's serfs. He felt close to the serf and to the Bishop who had covered him with his own cloak. How fatherly he had been! He had stood with Francis against his father, he had listened to Francis patiently when he had tried to explain about the dreams, the voices, the cross of San Damiano. He had welcomed Francis into the embrace of the Church.

And now years later, as Francis and the brothers plodded along in silence toward Assisi, he thought of Bishop Guido again, how it was he who, being in Rome when Francis and the brothers arrived, had intervened to procure an audience with Pope Innocent. Bishop Guido always seemed to be there when Francis needed him, seemed to understand that he and the brothers were about something new in the Church. Perhaps he was even proud of them for making his diocese of Assisi something to be noticed. But then the Bishop wouldn't have known that the first time Francis spoke with him. He would only have wondered about this strange son of Pietro Bernardone who was acting like some crazed fool of God begging stones to rebuild a church, talking of visions and voices. And yet he had listened. He seemed to understand, no matter what his reasons may have been.

And from what had happened in the Bishop's courtyard, he must have understood even better than Francis had dared imagine. The Bishop had sent him forth with his blessing. Like King Arthur, not knowing how his knight would fare, he trusted Francis's quest.

He remembered, too, how as he'd skipped playfully along the road to Gubbio, lost in his thoughts, he hadn't noticed the men following him. Perhaps it was because he had begun to sing in French, as he always did when he was happy.

Suddenly, he felt a heavy blow from behind and fell to the ground holding his head. When he looked up, menacing faces stood over him glaring.

"Who are you, imbecile?" one of them spat out.

"Singing in a secret tongue, are you, fool?" said another.

"Look at the fool, wearing a peasant's tunic with a cross chalked on it," the first voice said. The others laughed. "You're a singer, aren't you, down on your luck?"

He started to answer, but they set upon him before he could, searching him mercilessly for coins or anything valuable.

"So, you have nothing, you fool!"

"No," he managed to get out. "I am the herald of the Great King."

With that they began kicking him and roaring with laughter. "Herald of the Great King, are you?" And they dragged him to his feet and threw him into the ditch beside the road, leaving him writhing in pain and bleeding from his mouth and nose.

He lay there quietly, listening to their curses, their gruff voices receding in the distance. He felt his arms and legs, he began to move. He was okay, nothing seemed broken. He pulled some grass from the side of the ditch and stanched his mouth and nose.

Then something wonderful happened. He no longer was in pain. He stood up easily. He leapt from the ditch. He looked up to the sky and began to sing from his swollen mouth. He was singing the praises of the Great King whose vassal, Bishop Guido, had blessed his new life in the name of this King of all, the Lord and Creator—he, God's imbecile and herald—who even robbers recognized for who he was.

. . . .

Now as they approached the Valley of Rieti, halfway between Rome and Assisi, the brothers again shook him from his reverie, shouting and pointing to the town of Poggio Bustone high on a mountain ahead of them, and they all fell to their knees and remembered gratefully that precious mountain village and what had happened there to their father Francis and what God had told him about all of them and those who were to come after them.

His heart filled with gratitude at the very name, "Poggio Bustone." It was the site of his epiphany, for there as he and the brothers had made their way to Rome just a few weeks before, he knew again the Lord's mercy. For he had still been filled with guilt and a feeling of unworthiness as they walked to the Eternal City.

He had been plagued by a lingering feeling that the sins of his youth were so great that he would never be done with them. How could God forgive his selfishness and the blood lust of battle that made him do things he tried in vain to blot from his mind? How could God forgive the sins he remembered in kind and number? And even though he had confessed them and knew that he had been forgiven in the Sacrament, he could not forgive himself until that healing experience at Poggio Bustone.

There in that holy cave, as he was praying and bemoaning his sins and begging God's mercy, an unspeakable joy and sweetness began to flood his soul, and he knew his sins were forgiven. There was no voice, as at San Damiano. Instead he was caught up in a light that seemed to transport him beyond himself; so that he could see himself apart from himself, and he was forgiving himself. And inexplicably he let go of the past's hold on him.

He and the light were one, and he was having mercy on his own past, and he saw that the past was healed. But more was given him besides—the future; and it was this, more than anything, that gave him the confidence to know that their journey to Rome was not something only of his will, his dream. And he knew that Pope Innocent would receive them and would approve their Gospel way of life.

Again he had been caught up in indescribable light, and he saw a great host of men who were coming to share their life. The roads were filled with Frenchmen, Spaniards, Germans, Englishmen, and many others speaking different languages he'd never heard; and they were all hurrying toward him and the brothers.

And then the light lifted, and he was in the cave alone, and he rushed out and down the mountain to tell the brothers what God had let him see. They were to become many; they were to walk the roads of the world.

And now Francis and the brothers were again in Rieti, the charming valley surrounded by the Sabine Mountains. Here they would stay awhile preaching and helping the serfs work their fields. Here they would climb the mountainsides looking for places of solitude for prayer and contemplation.

How much a part of their lives was the solitude of this valley and these hills. Even on the way to Rome they had stopped every day when it was still light enough to climb up a hillside and find their separate places where they could pray apart and yet close enough to signal one another should they be in need of help or to warn of the danger of wild boars or robbers who lurked at times in the woods.

. . . .

Francis thought now of how, even before they went to Rome to seek the Pope's approval, the pattern of their lives had involved working in the fields, or wherever they were, to provide food should that be forthcoming; otherwise, they would beg—go to the Table of the Lord, as Francis had dubbed it. And they witnessed to their Lord and Savior Jesus Christ as they walked along the roads or worked with their hands. They found their separate caves or thickets in the woods at day's end where they could pray in secret as Jesus himself asked them to do when he said, "Whenever you pray, go into your room and shut the door and pray to your Father who is in secret; and your Father who sees in secret will reward you" (Matthew 6:6).

From the very beginning they had prayed like this. Even when he had first begun to seek out abandoned churches and mountain caves, Francis would pray to his Father in secret. And when he had renounced his father Pietro, praying to the Father became even more important because he needed to know that he still had a father.

When he left Assisi and fell among robbers, it was the Father he praised as he rose from the ditch and began to sing. And that first night on the way to Gubbio when, in the midst of a storm, he stopped at the Benedictine Monastery of San Verecondo and asked for shelter, even though he was rudely shuttled into the kitchen to wash the plates and pans and sleep in a corner of the room. He had found solitude in the cave he made of that corner. And when he left after a few days, the storm having subsided and knowing it was not the life of a monk he was called to, he found that he could withdraw to a cell within himself, as silent as a monk's cell, where he could pray to his Father in secret. And at his friend Federico's house, there, too, he found that cell within, even as he and Federico shared the same room.

It was in that cell that he found again the Father's will for him: that he should return to the Valley of Spoleto below Assisi where the lepers live and where he was to restore the little chapel of St. Mary of the Angels. This would be his Little Portion, his Porziuncola.

This is where he would find his Father's Son, Jesus, as he had found him while he was still in the world and heard him speak from the cross of San Damiano and when he saw him one day when he met a leper on the road.

It happened after he'd returned from Spoleto in shame, having left the other soldiers and his dream of knighthood in order to wait for what it was God would show him.

He was riding his horse, and seeing the leper, he was moved to rein in instead of racing by as he had in the past when he heard the leper's clapper or spied him shrinking to the side of the road, his head bowed, eyes cast down to the ground.

He stopped. He kept his eyes on the frightened leper. He dismounted and stood there wondering what he was doing. Then something moved him to reach for his purse, take out some coins and walk slowly to the leper in silence and fear. He reached out his hand and dropped the coins into the leper's bowl.

Then without thinking he impulsively embraced the startled leper, and feeling a sweetness of soul and body he'd never experienced before. All in silence. And in silence he turned away and mounted his horse. He turned again to wave to the leper— and there was no one there—and it entered his heart that he had embraced his Lord, Jesus Christ the Leper.

Then, in the silence of his own cell at Federico's house, he had known that this was what he was being shown according to the voice at Spoleto that said it would be shown him what he was to do: He was to go and live among the lepers in the swampy land below Assisi.

And this is what they would now tell the people of Rieti: God is where we least expect to find God. God is among those we despise or fear or find repulsive. God is a leper.

. . . .

The days in Rieti Valley were filled with light. Not just the stunning light that flooded this natural amphitheater surrounded by the Sabine Hills with Mt. Terminillo towering above them all, but the light that shone from the people, the serfs who like all peasants suffer so much at the hands of the nobles whose lands they work in a servitude not unlike that of slaves.

He thought of those who work his father's land and Bishop Guido's land below the walls of Assisi in the Spoleto Valley. He thought of how he had not even noticed them when he was a rich and spoiled young man.

And now these same people were ever on his mind. Ever since his encounter with the leper, he knew that they, the poor, are the face of Christ. And now he and the brothers, with the Pope's approval, were here to tell them how much God loves them, that of such as they is the kingdom of heaven, a kingdom that is all around them. Jesus himself had said, "Blessed are the poor in spirit, for theirs is the kingdom of heaven." Not, theirs *will be* the kingdom of heaven, but theirs *is* the kingdom of heaven. It is already theirs.

The brothers were there among them preaching also of virtues and vices, of punishment and glory, in few words because Jesus himself made his words brief when he was on earth. They had heard these words before, but now they were hearing them from those who were poor like them, those who were offering to help them by working together in their fields, sharing their meager meals with them.

And to the rich and noble they were preaching in like manner but as those who, like Christ, had emptied themselves of the riches and power and rank of some of their listeners, and they were claiming such power and honor as something not to cling to, as St. Paul says of Christ in his letter to the Philippians. They were warning the nobles of the dangers of appropriating to themselves what belongs to God alone.

The days passed quickly in this seemingly idyllic valley where the peasants, like peasants everywhere, suffer from the pride and arrogance and sometimes the cruelty of their lords.

But what rich soil was here for the seed of God's word. What flowering of faith and virtue! They preached, it seemed, all day long, not only in the city of Rieti but in the surrounding hill towns like Greccio and Francis's beloved Poggio Bustone. And they were listening to the brothers' words. How strange it must have seemed to them that God had chosen poor beggars, lower even than the serfs themselves, to preach the Gospel of Jesus Christ, beggars who had nothing but the poor tunics they wore and yet were obviously, some of them at least, men of previous power and influence; and one of them was even a priest of the Church. Imagine a priest who is a beggar!

Francis hoped they would go further and wonder, *Was Jesus himself like these men? Was Jesus like the serfs themselves?*

And so it had come to pass that this valley was the first place of sustained preaching by word and example for the newly approved band of poor, itinerant preaching brothers of penance. And it was good.

They were walking again now toward Assisi, toward the honeymoon God was surely preparing for them after their official wedding to Lady Poverty that took place in Rome's Church of St. John Lateran. They walked north, away from Rieti and Greccio and Poggio Bustone; away from Lake Piediluco toward the mountains. They walked and witnessed and worked for their food; and when they did not receive any food for their work in the fields, they begged from door to door, blessing those who opened their doors to them, whether or not they received any scraps from their table.

Francis was aware that they were a strange, perhaps frightening sight—twelve unkempt beggars walking purposefully along like a band of robbers. But he hoped their singing and their joy, the blessings they freely gave, and the courtesy of their manners and gentle speech disarmed the fear and hostility of the already downtrodden and abused serfs.

They would always greet whomever they met with, "The Lord give you peace," as Jesus had revealed to Francis that they should do. And they eagerly sought to help out in the fields or wherever they could help, not seeking money or alms in return, but hoping for food at the end of the day. And so it went, the daily trek back to Assisi, their hearts filled with joy that Jesus had shown his pleasure with them through his vicar, Pope Innocent.

The journey was long, but the time seemed short when one morning they saw the Valley of Spoleto open up before them with Mount Subasio in the distance shimmering through the mist. They had no home to return to but this place, this fair valley where Christ awaited them in the lepers.

They walked to where Francis knew there was an abandoned shed at Rivo Torto, named for the crooked stream that ran beside one of his own father's properties. It was an animal shed so small that Francis had to chalk the names of the brothers on the walls to indicate the place of each brother. How incongruous that the former son of the owner of property nearby was now to dwell in an abandoned shed for animals. How appropriate for those who walk in the footsteps of the Poor Savior. The shed shone with grace. It was indeed the chamber of Lady Poverty, the place where they would now lay their heads until God called them elsewhere.

They were tired. They lay down almost in a swoon and slept until the morning sun was already high in the sky. They rose like small animals from their nest, stretching and smiling when they realized where they were, this place where animals used to live, this place where God had led them. Francis knew that this would be where their true brotherhood would be fashioned. They had no permanent dwelling, but they had each other, the fraternity, and that was their dwelling place.

They went outside and greeted Brother Sun, and Francis led them in prayer.

· ·

How beautifully the days will unfold here, he thought, and always we will find food of some kind, not merely for ourselves, but for the lepers who live together in a community surrounding their small chapel of "La Maddalena," the Magdalen. They will be happy beggars. They will be serving the needs of Christ the Leper.

· ·

Leaving the hut at Rivo Torto was easy. They were driven out by an angry peasant looking for a place for himself and his donkey. But the leaving was also easy because leaving all cramped spaces was easy. Francis thought he knew why: prison—that of his father and of the Perugians. On the other hand, anything you cannot leave for reasons of comfort, or prayer or penance or any reason, is a prison. If you can leave and don't, you will remain imprisoned unless your very prison has become the open road itself. Then you would be escaping the prison by staying in the prison of your cell or cave.

· ·

Assisi had been a prison: its values, its constricted streets and walls, its greed, and its endless intramural battles. Always some family seemed to be warring against another. Or the nobles were fighting the merchants, or the commune was fighting the Bishop, or vice versa. Assisi became for him a prison of pettiness and violence and boredom.

How different it was now. He was outside the walls of Assisi and, more importantly, outside the walls of his own making: his vanity and love of fine things, his need to excel, to be the best knight, the best son, the leader of the other young men of the city. He had been brought down. He was finding another way where the way up was really the way down, as Jesus had come descended to show us how to rise.

And it had all begun and was drawn to a climax in his conflict with his father, Pietro, a conflict he never would have continued had not another Father drawn him. Perhaps he wouldn't even have been in conflict with his father in the first place but for the other Father in heaven.

He thought of the words of Jesus in the Gospel of John, 6:44: "No one can come to me unless drawn by the Father who sent me...." Was everything that began to happen when he determined to become a knight—the voices, the set-backs, the Perugian prison, his father's prison—all of it—the initial pull of the Father, drawing him to Jesus? And when he dismounted his father Pietro's horse to embrace Christ the leper, was not the Father exchanging Pietro's horse for the footsteps of his Son, Jesus?

If so, why did the Heavenly Father do this? Why was it necessary, or was it, that he renounce his father in order to find his Heavenly Father and his Son, Jesus Christ?

Francis could not reason this out satisfactorily. But, then, it was not about reason; it was about believing the words of Jesus: "Whoever comes to me and does not hate father and mother, wife and children, brothers and sisters, yes, and even life itself, cannot be my disciple"(Luke 14:26).

What does that mean? He could not hate his father and mother or his brother Angelo. Yet, that must surely seem to be what he had done when he chose the Father who was drawing him to Jesus.

All he knew was that this new Father was love, an all-giving love that invited the same total love from those who followed in the footsteps of his Son. And this new love was somehow a new love for his family, love not hate, though to those who knew neither the father nor the son it looked like hate and ingratitude.

He prayed that someday his mother Lady Pica and his father Pietro would be drawn by the same Father and would understand what their unpredictable son had done, how he'd become free in Christ as they, too, could become free in him who makes all things new, even family love and unpredictable sons.

Francis looked out onto the lands surrounding the Porziuncola. He thought of his youth and the time of the great famine which gripped his adolescence, the time when these lands did not yield, when the poor tenants, unable to pay their taxes, returned their lands to their masters, thus insuring the masters' increased wealth when the lands began to yield again. His own father Pietro gained more land during this time; and though the times were hard, he continued to travel to the cloth fairs of Champagne. Even in 1182, the year of Francis's birth, his mother seven months pregnant, his father left in July for Champagne.

Always it was that way when he was a boy. Wealth at home, poverty and misery on his father's lands below the city walls. And now he was here below the walls among the lepers, he and the brothers shuttling between the leprosarium at La Maddalena and their own matted huts at the Porziuncola a mile or so away.

The misery was still here, the wealth still above in the city where he was born and where some of the lepers were born, more than a few, perhaps, the same year as he. They, too, had had their dreams. And when was it they were found to be with leprosy? When were they banned from the city, given their clapper and bowl, told not to drink from wells, warned to clack their clapper when anyone appeared on the road they might be walking, and to cry aloud, "Unclean, unclean"? And sadly, how many were not afflicted with leprosy but with some other disease that looked like leprosy and caused them to be included among those living in the leprosaria?

And where was he when the liturgy of exclusion was held, when the leper put aside his or her fine or peasant's clothes, when the priest sprinkled black soil on his or her head and gave them the cloak and gloves of a leper? Where was he when a leper was given the leper's cell at the lepers' hospital and told that here was the leper's home until death?

He remembered the times he rode out of the city with his father on their way to the fairs of Champagne and would see lepers along the way pulling up their camel skin hoods and scurrying off the road into the woods, their clappers alive in their gnarled and fingerless hands.

He felt fear then. He prodded his horse to a faster trot, he set his sights on Champagne. There he would be in the light, in the festive exciting realm of Marie de Champagne, daughter of the great Lady, Eleanor of Aquitaine. There he would listen to the jongleurs singing the songs and tales of the Lady Marie's famous troubadour, Chretien de Troyes, who sang of King Arthur and the Knights of the Round Table. There he would begin to long for knighthood. And there his own songs would be loosed, and he would begin to sing in the langue d'oc, the language of the troubadours.

And where, when he was in Champagne, were the lepers his own age? Here. Here and in all the leprosaria of Umbria sitting in silence, unable to sing or even raise their heads in hope.

Here, then, he would sing for them and to them. He would bring the world of the troubadours to them, sing of another King, the Lord, not of the castle, but of the kingdom of heaven and earth. Their Lord, the One waiting for them at heaven's grand Round Table, waiting for them to return from this terrible Quest they were on, this heroic journey into sickness and disease, poverty and darkness, and the daily temptation to despair and curse their Lord, who sent them here.

Francis and the brothers would bring joy and hope and song. They would sing of the great King, who was also their

Shepherd and the Lamb who died for them. They would sing to the lepers of Jesus, who makes even a leprosarium a paradise of his heavenly court.

. . . .

THE YEAR OF OUR LORD 1212

Clare: Lady Poverty's Image

The sun was rising over Mount Subasio, its rays filtering through the mist that covered the Valley of Spoleto like a pillow of white feathers. The brothers were just finishing morning praise when Francis began to contemplate their future. What else was God asking of them? Already they were working in the fields helping the serfs, they witnessed to the Gospel in all seasons, and they ministered to the needs of the lepers.

But that sun—the way it broke through the morning mist and traveled across the valley and disappeared at evening, lighting and warming other lands until it returned—what was it saying to him this morning? What was it calling him and the brothers to so strongly this particular day?

He thought of the Bible and all the images of light there: of how God spoke to Moses in a burning bush, how God led his people by light both day and night as they made their way from Egypt to the Promised Land, how when they arrived in Jerusalem, God in the fullness of time led the Magi by means of a star to the New Jerusalem, the Light of the World, who was Jesus the Lord, King of heaven and earth.

In telling that story God told the whole story of creation from the time God created light out of darkness and separated the light from the darkness, to the final book of the Bible, the book of Revelation, through which Jesus gave us his final words: "It is I, Jesus who sent my angel to you with this testimony for the churches. I am the root and the descendent of David, the bright morning star" (Revelation 22:16).

That was the star that Francis and the brothers must follow if they were to fulfill Christ's words to him at San Damiano, "Go and repair my house." They were to live the Bible with poetry like that of the Bible, with songs and psalms; they were to travel and preach and witness to the Light who is Christ, thereby leading all they met along the way to the New Jerusalem in whom all will meet the living God.

But for now, they were to stay here awaiting the words of Christ who would show them where and how they were to go. That they were to go, Francis already knew. The words given him at the Porziuncola had begun with "Take nothing for your *journey.*"

He was sure, then, that they were being sent as the disciples were sent by Jesus two by two. The brothers were already doing as much and returning afterward to the Porziuncola. But were they doing enough, going out far enough?

Then, because his thoughts were contemplating with words and images from the Bible, and as the sun began to break through and scatter the mist, Francis knew that he must call all the brothers together at the Porziuncola to meet in Chapter. There they would pray for God's guidance as to how and where the journey with and toward the morning star would continue. Only the Holy Spirit could show them the way. They would meet on the Feast of Pentecost and again on the Feast of St. Michael the Archangel, the tutelary saint of chivalry.

Francis lifted his arms to the sun in—the sun, the great symbol of the Son of God.

But there was more to thank God for. In a few days, when the Sunday sun disappeared in the sky and all was deep darkness, another light would illumine the brothers' lives: Clare, the daughter of the Knight Favarone and his pious wife, Ortolana, descended from Charlemagne, would join the brothers at the Porziuncola.

Francis had been meeting with Clare secretly for over a year, and now just recently Bishop Guido told Francis that on Palm Sunday, as agreed upon by Clare, he was going to leave the altar and give a palm to the blessed Clare, instead of waiting for her to approach the altar like the other young women who, in all their finery, would walk to the altar for their palm hoping that they were catching the eyes of the available young men who would also be attending the services, friends and foes alike, for the first time after ten years of constant war.

The Bishop's gesture is to be Clare's sign that on that very Palm Sunday night, March 27, in the year of Our Lord 1212, she is to steal away from her home. Then Clare will come to the brothers at the Porziuncola. Francis is to cut off her hair and clothe her in the poor tunic of Lady Poverty. Then she will be led by the brothers to the Benedictine monastery at Bastia, where the nuns are to receive her temporarily until in the fullness of time Bishop Guido will give them the church of San Damiano for their permanent monastery.

How it warmed Francis's heart to know Clare's home would be San Damiano, the first church he repaired with his own hands. He remembered his own prophecy when he was restoring San Damiano. His Blessed Lord had told him that one day this building would be the home of Poor Ladies. And now it was coming to pass, stone by stone, slowly, just as he had repaired San Damiano, slowly, stone by stone.

Even the flickering candles seemed nervous with anxiety as the brothers waited for Clare, they hoped with her cousin Brother Rufino at her side. The plan was that Clare should escape from her home at the very heart of night and make her way through Assisi's darkened streets to the Porta Moiano, the city gate just below the walls of the Bishop's palace. Brother Rufino would be waiting just outside the gate.

And now they waited, Francis and the brothers. They waited and prayed Matins. As Brother Leo read the Second Nocturn Lesson, Francis knew this was indeed the day for Clare to join the brothers. The Reading was from the Sermon of St. Augustine on St. Mary Magdalene and how she dried the feet of Jesus with her hair. "The hair is nothing," Augustine wrote, "the feet of Jesus are essential." His heart leapt for joy as he thought of the feet of Jesus and how Clare would soon begin her life as a penitent, a servant of God, following in the footprints of the Lord at whose feet she would sit. The tonsure she would submit to would set her apart as one of them, one who is a servant of God alone.

The Divine Office completed, they went outside and again began to search the surrounding woods hoping to see the small flicker of Brother Rufino's torch as he and Clare made their way along the dark twists and turns of the path through the trees and underbrush. Seeing nothing but darkness, they began to sing the *Salve Regina*, their hymn to St. Mary of the Angels, the patroness of the chapel outside whose doors they huddled now in the chilly night air.

Francis knew that Clare would find a way out of one of the doors of her family home next to the church of San Rufino. But how would this young woman, merely nineteen years old, find the strength and stealth to unbar and push open the heavy door without being seen or heard? He knew she would. She had that in her which is the mettle of the saints and martyrs—that grace of purpose, that fortitude that would make her foundress of the Poor Ladies of San Damiano, the chapel he had restored with his own hands at Christ's command, "Go, repair my house which, as you see is falling into ruins." This determined young woman would keep it, he was sure, this chapel so dear to him. And she would keep it poor like her poor Spouse. Someone extraordinary was on her way to where the brothers stood shivering in the midnight air.

He had seen that exceptional mettle for months now as they spoke of Jesus whose spouse she was determined to be. They spoke of his radiant countenance shining from within the unexpected faces of the lepers down here below the city walls. They spoke of how it could happen that a woman, a noble woman, would ever be able to join the brothers. She insisted that God would show them the way.

And so it was coming to pass. With the knowledge and approval of good Bishop Guido, Clare had this very day, this Palm Sunday, gone with her parents to Mass at San Rufino. But instead of this day being her coming out presentation to the young men of Assisi gathered in the cathedral to look for possible future brides—as was the Palm Sunday custom— Clare was being presented to Christ in the person of Bishop Guido.

What must have been the consternation when Clare held back, refused to parade before the young men ogling the lavishly attired women who processed up the aisle to receive their palms, the hems of their bright and stunning dresses trailing possibilities. He wondered what her parents thought. Did they think she was ill, suddenly struck with an unwonted stage fright, or simply not ready for this? And how the whispering and tittering must have rushed through the church when the Bishop came down off the altar to where Clare sat and, inclining his head, placed the palm in her quivering hand, the sign and pledge of her pending betrothal to Christ!

Francis was sure that when their eyes met, Clare knew that Bishop Guido himself would see to her safety as she rustled stealthily through Assisi's streets from her father's house, through the Piazza Commune, along the street below where Francis's mother and father lay sleeping, and beyond that, to the Bishop's palace and the Porta Moiano.

If all of this did in fact happen, then now there was only the waiting. God's will was even now working the details of Clare's passage to the Porziuncola, the brothers' and her Little Portion, the chapel of St. Mary of the Angels. He and Clare had already worked it out that after he and the brothers had cut off her hair and clothed her in the habit of poverty, he and a few brothers would accompany her to the Benedictine monastery of San Paolo delle Abbadesse in Bastia, a short, two-mile walk from the Porziuncola. There the Abbess and nuns would offer her a temporary stay of five days before she was to go to Sant'Angelo in Panzo on Mount Subasio where there lived a group of penitent women. In the meantime Bishop Guido would be preparing San Damiano for Clare and whoever else would choose to join her there.

But all of these details, however important, were but human plans which, as he had learned so painfully, might unravel, or not be what God wanted. Christ himself would shepherd Clare. Christ would show her what it was hers to do.

And so they waited, praying and singing and looking for the smallest flicker of light beyond their own shortening candles. Clare. Chiara—herself a light that would light the Umbrian night where so many lay in darkness.

"There it is, see it? That flicker, just there." It was Brother Masseo speaking as all eyes turned to where his finger pointed.

"Yes, Father Francis. She is coming. Rufino found the way."

Francis, too, could see it now. A light shone on the path. Clare would now be one of them. And when Clare and Rufino emerged from the dark wood and wild, the brothers spontaneously broke into the song they'd sung earlier that day, "Holy, holy, holy. Blessed is He who comes in the name of the Lord, Hosanna in the Highest." A new light had dawned in the valley.

Her hair in his hands, her locks falling like petals onto the floor of the Porziuncola. How did this noble lady, with so many luxuries and possibilities of the world, arrive here? How could she allow a poor beggar to cut off her beautiful hair? And then allow brother after brother to cut another lock? And how did she find her way? Who opened the door of her parental home for her?

Jesus Christ. He is the door and the way. Even before this moment, before she came to talk with Francis, before her desire to join the brothers, Jesus was the door of her soul opening her to the way that is his very person. Francis had found that same door when he was in the prison of his own desires and ambitions; and walking up to it, he had seen that the door was Christ himself, the Way, the Truth, and the Life. And Francis himself strove to become in turn a door to the door who is Christ. The door was the way, and the way was the door.

And that is why Clare di Favarone was now kneeling before Francis and the brothers. They knew the way and the door, and she saw that in them, as they saw it in her. No door to possibilities was closed to her. Instead, the greatest possibilities were now open to her, and she was saying yes, as Francis now clothed her in the garment of Lady Poverty, a raiment as poor and rich as Jesus Christ, who, like her, had emptied himself, becoming obedient to the Father's will, and who had thereby become the fullness of riches that would continue to attract those who could see. What was being enacted here was a mystery the door to which was Christ alone. It was the way hidden from the eyes of those who cannot embrace the mystery.

What else could Clare do, but kneel before the magnitude of it all? She did not kneel to him and the brothers but to what she saw in them, the Door and the Way. Even her hair falling to the floor was more than hair falling to the floor. What a mysterious falling and rising was here! This would be the pattern of all their lives, and it would begin now as together they made their way to Bastia, a way that would end and begin at San Damiano where her door would again open from the cross, "Go and repair my house which, as you see, is falling to ruins."

Proclaiming the Nearness of God

And then there was the time of doubt about the direction his life should take. More and more brothers were entering the fraternity, and the pattern of their lives was slowly being established. Francis himself was deeply drawn to a life of prayer, and he wondered if he and the brothers should focus their lives more on prayer and contemplation. Was that the direction God was now giving them?

As was his practice, he turned to others for their advice, lest his own selfishness interfere with God's will and assert itself and convince him that what he was most drawn to was probably what God wanted of him. So he sent Brother Masseo to inquire of Brother Sylvester and Sister Clare if they would ask God what he and the brothers should do.

Brother Sylvester was a priest who spent long periods of time on Mount Subasio; and when he heard Francis's request, he turned immediately to God in prayer. And God answered, "Brother Francis, the Lord says that he has not called you to this state only for yourself, but that you might reap a harvest of souls and that many souls might be saved through your preaching and example." And Sister Clare received the same answer in prayer.

He would continue, then, as he had done from the beginning, preaching and witnessing to the Gospel, and, like Jesus himself, taking time to go apart and pray. For everything that God had done through Francis and the brothers began in prayer and led into further prayer. That balance—praying on the mountain or in the woods, and witnessing on the road. And that was why he was here now praying on Mount Subasio, but knowing that he could not stay here forever.

In the valley and part way up the mountain where Assisi lay sprawled on the mountain's spur, a giant cloud had settled, a huge, white, puffy cloud. It was early morning, and little by little openings occurred, and he could see the green verdure peeping through.

Often when he was praying like this on the mountain, he too would be inside a cloud that had settled over the mountain. It made him think that perhaps prayer itself was like learning to live inside a cloud that kept him and the brothers from seeing into the mystery so that they had to wait patiently for the cloud to disperse and reveal what was as near as the cloud that kept them from seeing it.

God was continually renewing the world but they couldn't see that re-creating work because of the cloud they were living in—though every once in a while something would break the cloud cover, and they'd see that the cloud was the very God they were expecting to break through the clouds. What broke through was God's work done in what seemed only cloud that needed to lift before they could see.

But too much of this kind of thinking, he realized, does

nothing but turn us away from the footprints of Jesus that are imprinted in the very soil where we live. However cloudy that soil may be, we know the footprints are there where Jesus said they would lead: to those who are hungry and thirsty, to the stranger, the naked, the sick, and those in prison. There was nothing cloudy about Jesus's words: the footprints led to Jesus himself, even though at times Francis felt he was walking in a cloud toward a cloud.

For him the clarity was not in what he saw and embraced, but in how he saw by means of Jesus's own words. Sometimes he saw, sometimes he didn't, that it was Jesus he'd met, and he was saying, "I was hungry and you gave me food, I was thirsty and you gave me something to drink, I was a stranger and you welcomed me, I was naked and you gave me clothing, I was sick and you took care of me, I was in prison and you visited me" (Matthew 25:35–37).

These words made everything clear for him, and living them, even when God seemed distant or an enveloping cloud, brought near the kingdom of God. That is what the brothers' lives had proven from the very beginning: Though prayer may seem like a cloud, at times, living the Gospel revealed to them the kingdom of God.

"The kingdom of God has come near." This one sentence from St. Luke's Gospel rang in his ear whenever he was tempted to settle down into too comfortable a life of prayer and solitude. It appears when Jesus is talking to his disciples, sending them out in pairs to every town and place where he intended to go. He says to them,

Whenever you enter a town and its people welcome you, eat what is set before you; cure the sick who are there, and say to them, "The kingdom of God has come near to you." But whenever you enter a town and they do not welcome you, go out into its streets and say, "Even the dust of your town that clings to our feet, we wipe off in protest against you. Yet know this: the kingdom of God has come near." (Luke 10:8–11)

That movement, that going forth to proclaim by word and healing that the kingdom of God has come near is what had kept the brothers from growing complacent. They would be received, they would be rejected, but whatever the case, they would be continuing their vocation to bring near the kingdom of heaven.

True, they could die proclaiming and living love by binding up wounds and embracing the poor and rejected ones, but that is the nature of love: to die, if need be, for others. It is the nature of darkness, on the other hand, to sit back complacently and watch others die.

In bringing near the kingdom of heaven the brothers were engaging in one of the oldest of dramas in which the battle between darkness and light is played out. It was not so much a battle in which they fought the darkness, as it was the ongoing battle with themselves to keep bearing the light, to keep bringing near the kingdom and not giving up, even when they were rejected. For even in rejection they are bringing near the kingdom. And even if they were martyred for proclaiming these words of Jesus, they were not overcome by darkness; they were yielding to the light.

To keep bearing the light, even to the point of martyrdom. That was what the itinerant life was: walking the roads of the world proclaiming that the kingdom of God has come near. And when you were rejected, you did not then yield to darkness, but you proclaimed the light once more and moved on.

This was their life, those whom God had given him as brothers.

And their numbers were growing. Men young and old had begun to come to Our Lady of the Angels drawn by God who had found them ready, as Francis himself had been ready. Their previous lives had come to nothing, and God knew they were ready to listen to Love, to the Shepherd seeking his lost sheep.

God led them to the Porziuncola, the Little Portion, that they hoped would fill all their needs. It was more than a place; it was a choice, a commitment to a poverty rich in the fullness of grace and brotherhood. He knew Christ was their Shepherd and his Holy Spirit their wisdom and light, and so Francis wasn't worried about what they were to eat or where they were to sleep or how they were to be clothed. Their Shepherd knew what they needed and would show them the way—provided, of course, that they chose the Lady Poverty for their bride as he and the first brothers had. She was their Little Portion leading to the land of the living; she was the way to Christ.

Nor was Francis concerned about what they were to do. They would send each other forth, as Christ had sent the disciples forth, two by two, to announce the Good News by their manner of living and how they related to one another and how they greeted others and told them of God's love and the need for conversion of heart by which they would turn and become like children again. And they would work with their hands and bless on their way all those who shared their food.

It was all quite simple once they were ready to hear the Gospel and live it out. Their lives would then be images of the Gospel itself. He thought of Jesus, who before he ascended into heaven, had said to his disciples the words that Francis had taken as central to their very way of life:

> All authority in heaven and on earth has been given to me. Go therefore and make disciples of all nations, baptizing them in the name of the Father and of the Son and of the Holy Spirit, and teaching them to obey everything that I have commanded you. And remember, I am with you always, to the end of the age. (Matthew 28:18–20)

That was how they were to live their lives, and they would do it by being poor like Christ, by being men of the road like Jesus and his Apostles, by preaching God's word as Jesus did, by being brothers to one another, to others, and to all creatures, and by the penance of their lives, emptying themselves for love of him who had emptied himself for love of them. And all of it flowed in and out of prayer, the prayer of the mountain, sometimes in a cloud, sometimes in light, but always clear in what it moved them to do once they left the mountain.

And so it was that at the first Chapter when hundreds of brothers came together and confessed their sins to one another, Francis sent them forth beyond the environs of Assisi to all of Italy, to Spain and Portugal, to France and Germany, and even to Morocco to preach and witness among the Muslims there.

They were to model their lives on the life of Jesus and of his Apostles. And so, there would be movement in their way of life as they brought the Gospel to others, but there would also be daily times of prayer and contemplation. They would leave the road each day and retire to a mountain or places of solitude like abandoned churches where Christ would reveal to them his will and where their souls could be renewed in Christ's Spirit. Theirs was an intimacy with Christ fostered in prayer and shared and strengthened through itinerant preaching.

Francis marveled at how like the life of Christ in St. Mark's Gospel was their own way of life. He loved especially the first chapter of St. Mark's Gospel which showed them so clearly what they were to do. It begins with a passage from the prophet Isaiah:

> "See, I am sending my messenger ahead of you, who
> will prepare your way, the voice of one crying out

in the wilderness: 'Prepare the way of the Lord.'"
(Mark 1:2–3)

And then Jesus was baptized by John who was that baptizer
who had prepared the way for Jesus.

> And as Jesus came up from the water, the Spirit
> descended upon him, and a heavenly voice
> proclaimed, "You are my Son, the Beloved; with you
> I am well pleased." (Mark 1:11)

Then the Spirit led Jesus into the wilderness for forty days.
And though he was tempted by Satan, he remained among
the wild beasts, and angels ministered to him.

> And when John was arrested, Jesus came to Galilee
> proclaiming the Good News that "the time is
> fulfilled, and the Kingdom of God has come near;
> repent and believe in the good news." (Mark 1:15)

These passages from St. Mark were for Francis the beginning and end of the brothers' mission. Like John (and Jesus
after him) they must first go into the desert of prayer and
fasting before they dared prepare the way of the Lord. They
were to do so in order that those who heard would be led to
Baptism or to renew their Baptism and in their own rising
from the water would meet Christ and know that, yes, this is
God's Beloved Son.

Then when the brothers moved on, Jesus himself would
begin to reveal to people the kingdom of God that had come

near them. And the brothers would continue to retire to the desert where they would be tempted and tried and then return to affirm in their preaching that the kingdom of God had indeed drawn near. They would preach to those who had already heard and to those who were new listeners in new towns and cities and byways.

All their lives then, the brothers' and those who heard them, would consist in unfolding and uncovering the life of Jesus in them, from the beginning of his public life until he was taken up into heaven.

The brothers were to show the people again and again that the life of Jesus was being re-lived in them. If they were suffering, they were suffering in and with Christ; if they were joyful, Christ himself was being joyful in them; if they were praying, Christ's Spirit was praying in them; if they were dying, they were dying with and in Christ; and when they died, they would rise with Christ.

What that meant in their concrete, everyday lives, was spelled out by St. Mark in his Gospel, the shortest of the Gospels. St. Mark made his words short because Jesus himself made his words short since he, like the brothers, was mostly on the road when he preached and taught.

That is why Francis would repeatedly say to his brothers, "Go then, my brothers; you go to meet Christ who himself sent you to meet him along the way of prayer and the way of witnessing the Gospels to others, as the Lord himself revealed to Brother Sylvester and Sister Clare that we should do."

THE YEAR OF OUR LORD 1219

The Peace-Maker

All the brothers were again gathered around his beloved Porziuncola, the small stone chapel Francis had restored with his own hands. They had come from far and near for their annual General Chapter, which was held on the Feast of Pentecost. "The Holy Spirit," he had told his brothers, "is the real Minister General of the Order." God's Spirit would now show them what they were to do.

. . . .

Francis thought of Jesus, how he did not shrink from teaching in the temple, in the marketplace. How, even as a boy, he sat among the elders and teachers of the law and listened to them. He spoke to them in words the Father sent him to speak. Jesus was like a Knight of the Heavenly Round Table; and the Father was the great King who sent his own Word who was Jesus to speak the truth, to heal, to proclaim the kingdom of God. Jesus was the Knight of Reconciliation bringing together by his words and life the fragmented languages of the Tower of Babel.

That is why Francis wanted to join Jesus by walking in his footsteps, witnessing to his Way, his Truth, his Life. Francis wanted to go to the court of the Sultan to witness to Christ while he also listened to the Sultan witnessing to Islam.

He knew many of the brothers would criticize and judge him for his presumption and pride in wanting to go into the court of the Sultan and speak with him, but years before he had gone to the lepers and found there, in that unexpected place, the court of the Lord Jesus Christ and Jesus himself waiting for him there. That was surely what he would find this time if he dared to seek God in an unexpected place.

. . . .

And so it came to pass that when the brothers did indeed vote to expand their missionary journeys, he asked to be sent to Damietta in Egypt at the mouth of the Nile River. The Crusaders were encamped there, preparing to set siege to the Muslim fort commanded by Sultan Malik al-Kamil. God had revealed to Francis that if the Crusaders decided to attack the Sultan, they would be defeated, and he was keen on conveying that message to them.

Perhaps he could do so by sharing God's message with the Italian Crusader Knights and soldiers he would embark with, reinforcements on their way to the Christian camp in Damietta.

They were to embark at Ancona on the Adriatic Sea east of Assisi, then sail to the Italian port of Bari in the kingdom of Sicily just north of Brindisi, the point of departure for Candia, Rhodes, and Damietta. If all went well, they would cross the mouth of the Adriatic to Corfu and continue south along the Balkan peninsula to Crete and from there to Rhodes where they would make the few days' journey across the open water of the Mediterranean Sea to Damietta. That, at least, was the plan as explained to Francis and the brothers when they arrived by foot in Ancona.

The journey from Ancona to Bari to Brindisi was relatively short, but it was enough time for most of the brothers to get used to the ship. He was allowed to take with him only a few brothers because of the crush of passengers making the journey. Among them were Brothers Illuminato, Peter Catanii, and Bernard of Quintavalle. Peter and Bernard had been with him when he asked the priest to open the Missal of Assisi's Church of San Nicolo, and they had read there, in three separate openings, that they were to give away all they owned and follow in the footsteps of the Poor Christ. Then there was Illuminato the Brave. He had been born blind but gained his sight through the mercy of God and the prayers of Francis and the brothers.

When they first set sail, Francis prayed more intensely than usual for all on board the ship that God would grant them safe passage because he had suffered through a merciless storm in his previous attempt to sail to the Holy Land seven years before. That time, before they could sail south, a fierce storm had blown them violently northeast toward the coast of Dalmatia, where they were cast up onto the shore, unable to resume their voyage.

On that aborted voyage Francis had kept St. Paul in mind, praying to God through Paul's intercession who had survived three shipwrecks and had been adrift on the sea for a night and a day.

This present voyage from Ancona to Brindisi was uneventful, except for the swearing and carousing of the soldiers and the company of a young cleric who befriended them, a scholar bound for Acre in the Holy Land to serve in the household of Jacques de Vitry, Bishop of Acre.

When they left Brindisi, the seas were calm and the young cleric pointed out to them the pillars that the great Latin poet Virgil wrote of. He was about to say more when the ship left the harbor into open water and began to rock back and forth and up and down.

One of the sailors cautioned everyone that they were heading into a storm and they should keep their eyes on the horizon to prevent sea sickness.

Soon a few, including Brother Leonardo and Brother Barbaro, turned pale and tried to vomit over the side of the ship, only to have the sickening vomit blow back onto them and others. More and more became sick, and the deck turned to a gooey mess that the sailors tried in vain to mop up.

For two days the storm raged but mercifully the wind was from the northwest and kept pushing the boat south toward Corfu. He thought of the words from Habakkuk's "Canticle."

> You trampled the sea with your horses
> churning the mighty waters,
>
> I hear, and I tremble within;
> my lips quiver at the sound.

(Habakkuk 3:15–16)

Both days Francis kept his eyes on the horizon till nightfall when he tried to lie down and sleep, his eyes fixed on Jesus walking toward him on the horizon and never arriving, as in a dream.

He woke in the second watch of the night, the creaking of the ship in his ears and the brothers all huddled near him. At first he had feared for them, what they'd be forced to see in the cramped and fetid spaces below decks. *Scenes of his year in prison flashed before him: the acrid odors of excrement and unwashed bodies, the rats and rot, and the dank air of confined spaces.* But they, like him, were men schooled in Christ, and they had lived lives of conversion and penance. They were not children.

They had all been tempted variously and known the victory of grace within them. They had learned to keep their eyes fixed on the Lord Jesus, who now consoled Francis as he thought of Jesus scourged by crude soldiers who mocked and spit upon him. Like a lamb he had been led to slaughter, innocent and pure, though all around him Jesus saw the effects of sin and surrender to instincts that in their baseness must have broken the heart of Jesus who saw into their souls and knew who they could have become.

Only Jesus could help Francis and the brothers huddled and sleeping around him from becoming again what they once had been before they knew the love and intimacy of God made real in Jesus. He closed his eyes and imagined Jesus sleeping with them as in the boat with his Apostles, a man like them whose Spirit breathed them all into a peaceful sleep. He began to surrender again to sleep, to the rhythm of Jesus's breath sleeping with them. He knew that in the morning the same Spirit would lift their hearts in prayer until at last they beheld the blessed land where Jesus had walked and preached before them. How far, he wondered, was Damietta from the Jerusalem he now began to dream?

One morning he saw water birds and knew that land was near, though there was, as yet, only the same relentless water on the horizon. By noon, the sailors told them, land would suddenly emerge as if rising from the sea.

And so it happened, and so they came at last to Acre, the Christian port northwest of Jerusalem, and from there Francis and the brothers traveled to Damietta in Egypt. It was the thirteenth year of Francis's conversion.

The Sultan frowned, surprised that the Crusaders would send two such obvious spies as seeming messengers of peace. And he said as much to them. Francis remembered much of that first interview, just as the image of Damietta was still strong in his mind. Even for one who grew up in Assisi, a walled city with many towers, one who was a prisoner in the walled city of Perugia and who had seen the towers of Rome, the port city of Damietta was a striking sight when it finally came into view. The port frontage on the River Nile was protected by two rows of walls that circled the city with forty-two bastions. Facing the land was a third wall with twenty gates and a moat so wide it could be patrolled by a galley. And shining in the sunlight above the workshops and warehouses were a hundred towers, one of which was the great mosque. This was the heavily protected city that he and Illuminato were allowed to enter after much roughing up and abusive shouting.

The Sultan, Malik al-Kamil, was a towering man who exuded power and authority, a match for any of the Crusader Knights. His eyebrows were thick but smooth and somehow delicate in their framing of his dark, penetrating eyes. His beard was full and matted with twisted curls that made him look very complicated: smooth eyebrows, twisted beard. Though powerfully wrought, there was something almost genteel about him, like Francis's dream of what a knight should be. His dark skin shone with a sheen of oil that seemed applied, giving him a handsome, almost royal aura. No wonder this man had been knighted by Richard the Lionhearted when al-Kamil was but eleven years old as a gesture toward peace in negotiations between Richard and Malik's father, the Muslim leader, Al-Adil.

Al-Kamil looked amused as Francis and Illuminato stood before him. He was looking at their feet, battered and encrusted with dirt that they had tried in vain to wash off before entering the Sultan's camp.

"You have tough feet, strong, road worn. I'm encouraged because without those feet, even though you're dressed like beggars, you could have been soft spies. You still could be spies. Are you beggars or are you spies sent from the Crusaders' camp?"

Francis loved it that the Sultan had noticed their feet. He noticed things.

"We are beggars, mighty Sultan, but we are spies, too. God's spies."

Malik al-Kamil smiled.

"I thought you would be the one to speak. My guards told me you gave your companion orders when they roughed you up. You spoke with authority. And, I see, you are clever with words that are simple, simple words that are clever but not arrogant."

"Great Sultan, we are simple. But we are neither clever nor arrogant. We are honest men who make our words simple like those of him who sent us." "And who is it, then, who sent you? What Lord or ruler? Can it be the indomitable, crafty, deceitful Cardinal Pelagius?"

"I know not if the Lord Cardinal is deceitful, but he is not the one who sent us. No, great Sultan, the Lord is Our Lord and Savior Jesus Christ."

"Then you've answered my second question already: You are not here hoping to convert to Islam."

"On the contrary, we are here to bring you to God in Jesus Christ."

"So. You are not warriors then, but Christian monks wandering outside your monastery, trying to convert the enemy with words disrespectful of Allah and Islam? There is no God, there is no Lord but Allah, beggar. Be careful of what you say in our presence. But this Jesus Christ. We know him, of course, one of the prophets of Allah, like Muhammad. You have mistaken the messenger for the Lord, who is Allah alone, though his names are many. By the way, beggar, one of Allah's names is not Jesus Christ!"

"Forgive me, good Sultan, for correcting you, but we are not monks. We are poor, itinerant, preaching brothers of penance sent by the Church of Rome to bring the Gospel of Jesus Christ to all those we meet along the way. For us Jesus Christ is the only Son of God, and in the deepest mystery, Jesus Christ *is* God. That is why they call us Christians. We believe that Jesus Christ is God."

The collective gasp was audible. This was something the Sultan knew, but what shocked everyone there is that Francis had dared to utter the truth of his faith so blatantly in the presence of the Sultan. Francis knew he was treading on a delicate membrane of the Muslim faith. And the flash of anger in the Sultan's eyes, momentary though it was, told him that the martyrdom he sought in Morocco might greet him here in the court of the Sultan Malik al-Kamil. He dared to continue, praying that God would give him the words.

"I'm only telling you what we believe, great Sultan, in order to witness to who we are and so that you can tell us who you are."

Silence. Everyone was waiting to hear what the Sultan would say.

"Leave us! I will speak to this beggar with the cracked and caked feet alone. You, beggar, tell your companion to wait outside with the others."

And they were left alone in the tent.

And so began what Francis had prayed would happen. He met Jesus in an unexpected man, the "enemy," like the lepers who also were considered the "enemy." He and the Sultan shared their faiths, their hope for peace, and became in the end friends. What they said to one another was their secret, except for what al-Kamil said to him when he left: "Pray for me, holy beggar, that Allah will reveal to me the law and the faith that is more pleasing to him."

Then when Francis and Illuminato were given safe passage back to the Crusader camp, both Muslim soldiers and Crusaders looked upon them with contempt and suspicion, as those who do not understand always do. Francis thought of Jesus preaching and healing and the Scribes and Pharisees watching him, looking for a way to silence him and get rid of him.

But some who saw Francis and Illuminato walk into camp smiled, and the brothers were eager to hear what had happened and whether or not the Sultan had been converted? But Francis only said that what had been repulsive to him before was now turned to the joy of finding a way toward peace between Christians and Muslims and a way of living together in harmony.

He could see that this puzzled the brothers, but he needed time to sort it out himself. When he returned to Assisi, he would write letters that would include everything good he had learned that Islam shared with Christianity and Christianity with Islam.

Just then a bell rang, and Francis fell prostrate to the ground and invited the brothers to do the same. He had learned that during those days with Sultan Malik al-Kamil when he heard the summons of the muezzin five times a day and saw the soldiers and all at court fall to the ground in complete obedience to the Creator and Ruler of the universe; and with a ritual of postures and movements, called the salat, they would render praise to Allah, the Merciful and Gracious, the Compassionate. When he returned to Italy, if that should be God's will, he would encourage Christians to praise God whenever the bells are rung. If it is God's will, "inshallah," as the Muslims would say, if it pleases Allah.

How strange, yet how fitting and natural, that Christians and Muslims alike sought to know and surrender to the will of God/Allah. Different names, the same God. What are names anyway, he wondered? The Ninety-Nine Names of Allah, or the many names for God in the Bible. The names define and describe God while God is beyond all names, ineffable and unknowable, unseeable, except by faith. "I will hide my face from them," God says in Deuteronomy (32:20). But that face for Francis was again revealed in Jesus, God's Word made flesh. And that face "shone like the sun…and from the cloud a voice said, 'This is my Son, the Beloved; with him I am well pleased; listen to him'" (Matthew 17:2, 5). That is the face of God that Francis tried to show the Sultan, a face the Sultan could not see, for the eyes of his faith were elsewhere—on the names of God that revealed Allah's countenance to him.

The uniqueness of Christianity struck Francis deeply in that only here, in his faith, did the names and words of God become flesh. That was his faith, a faith the Sultan could not share. What they could share, and did, was prayer that the will of God would be revealed to them from within their separate faiths. For each the religion of the other was false, but the will of God transcends religions, reaching down even to those of faiths other than one's own and to non-believers, like the oriental chieftain, Job the Great, Job who lived in the land of Uz, a man good and upright, a man who feared God and turned away from evil, a man whose very name meant "enemy."

He and Illuminato had been guests of the Sultan for almost two weeks, and from time to time he and the Sultan would talk. He remembered one such encounter especially. Sultan al-Kamil was intent on giving Francis lavish gifts of gold, silver, and silk garments as a parting gesture of their encounters. When Francis protested, the sultan said they could be given to the poor; but Francis saw the trap in that for him. It would make him think and perhaps act as if material things were the gifts the brothers had to offer.

They would not be able to say with St. Peter, "I have no silver or gold, but what I have I give you; in the name of Jesus Christ of Nazareth, stand up and walk" (Acts 3:6).

When he told the Sultan this, Brother Illuminato, the Brave Enlightened One, broke in.

"Yes, great Sultan. Yes. I myself was healed of blindness—I was born blind—by the prayers of our Father Francis. That is why I am here today, your Sultanship." (Here the translator stumbled, but whatever he came up with, it made al-Kamil laugh.)

Francis smiled, pleased that Illuminato had gained the courage to interrupt Francis and speak about this extraordinary miracle. Francis wanted to protest Illuminato's belief that it was Francis's prayers that healed him rather than Jesus himself, but that would surely seem like false humility and would detract from Illuminato's own witness to the truth he believed in. After all, wasn't that what they had been about for days now, listening to what one another believed?

Illuminato's face shone, a proof that he, too, stood in a truth that had changed his life. The Sultan praised Allah, the Merciful, the Compassionate.

Then al-Kamil asked if Francis would at least accept an honorary token of their friendship, a beautiful ivory horn.

"Dear friend, you honor me and all the brothers, and we thank you for such generosity and thoughtfulness. I accept your gift with pride. I know such horns are often used to announce battles, but I will use it to announce our arrival whenever we preach the Gospel of Jesus Christ."

"Thank you, Francis the Beggar, for the honor you bestow on me in receiving this small gift. It will, I see, do good."

Then, surprising himself with the words God put into his mouth, Francis said, "I am glad you understand that we cannot receive rich gifts, but I would like to ask for one more small gift."

"Say the word, Francis of God. What is it?"

"I would like for my brother Illuminato and me to share a farewell meal with you. It would honor our whole brotherhood."

Nothing could have made al-Kamil happier. He knew how the leaders of the Christian Church frowned on Christians sharing a meal with Muslims, but he also knew that nothing would seal their friendship and mutual respect more tangibly than sharing a meal together.

"The honor is mine, friend."

And so the Sultan and his court and the two brothers sat down to a lavish banquet that started with a kind of unleavened bread and a dip in which Francis tasted eggplant, ground and toasted walnut, and raw onion. The main course, served on a large gold platter, was a cooked dish of lentils and lamb in a sauce of exotic spices that Francis couldn't identify. It was served with rice.

In addition to water two drinks were served. One was a sweet mint drink and the other a lemon drink, both made, it seemed, from a sugary syrup. For dessert there was a platter of pastries and sweets. One was a pastry made with flour and sesame oil stuffed with almonds, sugar, and rosewater. Another consisted of little balls made of dates, ground nuts, breadcrumbs, and butter. There were also candies made of what tasted like honey, almonds, and sesame oil.

Both Francis and Illuminato loved the food and rejoiced in the abundance of it and the different tastes and smells, all of which they could partake of because everything God made is good, and the brothers were used to partaking of whatever was set before them, whether a tasty meal or a bowl of slop that they received when they went begging.

Though it wasn't supposed to be done, Francis knew that

this eating sociably with Muslims made Jesus smile; for he too had eaten with those whom others considered sinners and enemies.

The only edge of sadness came at the end of the meal when the Sultan offered Francis a visit to the Holy Sepulcher in Jerusalem, and he had to say no, knowing that Pope Honorius had barred Christians, under pain of excommunication, from visiting shrines under Muslim control. And he would obey the Pope as the Brothers' Rule required.

It wasn't hard to decline this offer, for Jesus, too, strove to obey every jot and tittle of the Jewish law. We grow, Francis thought, when we submit our will to the Church's will, as long as it is not against our conscience and our Rule.

It was after sharing that lovely meal that he and Illuminato left the Sultan and were accompanied to the Crusader camp by the Sultan's hand-picked guards. And as the two brothers walked out of the camp, they did not shake the dust from their feet. For though the Sultan had not been converted, he had listened and debated, especially during the Friday night debates before the whole court that al-Kamil so delighted in.

Francis and Illuminato had been received graciously by this great man who was known among the Christians of Egypt as the most tolerant and benevolent of the sultans. At this thought, Francis, as he had played an imaginary violin when he was happy, now blew a real ivory horn and announced to all accompanying the brothers that God had visited Damietta.

THE YEARS OF OUR LORD
1221–1223

The Shepherd, The Lamb, and the Baby

These were the hardest memories. The resumption of the war, the Christian siege and taking possession of Damietta, its residents either dead in the streets or dying from the stench of rotting bodies and from starvation; and the Crusaders mercilessly sacking the city, taking gold, silver, silk, pearls, and gold thread, even though they had sworn under pain of excommunication not to pillage the city. He mourned for all who had died, Crusaders and residents of the city, and he mourned for his friend Malik-al Kamil who had sued for peace five times and in the end was defeated by war itself, as were the Crusaders, many of whom lost their souls to greed and violence and lust.

Francis turned his face to Acre, his eyes aching from a painful disease that had developed when he was in Damietta. He had preached the Gospel in Acre for several months, trying at the same time to recuperate from his painful eye illness. And then he heard the news. Five of the six brothers he had sent to Morocco had been beheaded because of their insistence on preaching the Gospel no matter how many times they were asked not to; and even after they had been shipped to the port city of Ceuta where they were supposed to board ship for home, they refused to leave or stop preaching, and in the end they were tortured and then beheaded by Sultan Abu-Jacob himself. Francis hoped that they had laid down their lives not only for Christ but for the Sultan's salvation, too, and for the conversion of the people of Morocco. He could still see them bravely leaving the Porziuncola: Berard, Peter, Adjuto, Accursio, Otto, and Vitale. They were so young and inexperienced, but Vitale was put in charge and would bring prudence, Francis thought, to this first missionary journey to Islam. But Vitale, it seemed, never reached Morocco, having become ill in Spain. So now they had five martyrs, five who had witnessed to the Gospel even unto death.

Francis thought immediately of Sultan Malik al-Kamil and how reasonable he had been and how Francis and Illuminato tried to dialogue and not preach; how the sultan had listened and how he had debated with Francis and Illuminato. Francis would write a new chapter in his Rule on how the brothers are to go among the Muslims and other non-believers. They could either go and live among them witnessing by their lives to the faith they lived; or, if it was God's will, they could preach the Gospel when God showed them that is what they were to do. He wrote it in his mind so that Brother Leo could copy it down when he returned to Assisi.

You can live spiritually among nonbelievers in two ways. One way is not to enter into arguments or disputes but for the sake of the Lord to be subject to every creature (1 Peter 2:13) and to acknowledge that you are Christians. Another way is to proclaim God's word when you see it is pleasing to the Lord, so that those who do not believe may believe in the all-powerful God—Father and Son and Holy Spirit—Creator of everything, and in the Son who is Redeemer and Savior, and so that they may be baptized as Christians; for "no one can enter the kingdom of God without being born through water and the Spirit." (John 3:5)

Francis was both saddened and full of joy, saddened because the brotherhood had lost five brothers, all of whom were dear to him, but joyful, too, because they preached the Gospel to the point of death. But not all of the brothers would long for martyrdom the way these brothers had, and so it would be necessary to show the brothers a way of spiritual martyrdom by simply living among non-believers and standing in the truth of who they are, even in the face of insult and taunting, torture, or even death should that be God's will and not their own.

This shocking news, though, was not as terrible as the news that followed close upon this great sacrifice that was not unlike that of the Lamb of God. The terrible news was that some of the brothers, and even the two brothers put in charge of the brotherhood when he was away in the Holy Land, had betrayed Christ himself. They had insulted his Bride, the Lady Poverty, by building houses to live in.

He and Peter Catanii had just sat down to eat when Brother Stephen arrived from Assisi. Breathless, he stammered out that Brother Matthew of Narni and Gregory of Naples, the two vicars Francis had appointed in his absence, had allowed the brothers to build dwellings for themselves, and one of these buildings in Bologna was to be used as a house of studies for the brothers.

His heart sank. He could not believe these two brothers would violate these fundamental principles of their Rule that the brothers were to be poor and humble having no dwelling they could call their own, and that they were not to be learned brothers with their own study houses like the monks and Dominicans.

Stephen even hinted that new rules were being legislated in which they were not to eat meat. Francis had always insisted that the brothers were not to exclude any food the Lord had provided for them; they were to eat of whatever was placed before them, not separating foods as good or bad the way some were wont to separate people and divide people and label some "bad" or "enemy." Such elitism smacked of the Albigensian heretics who believed meat was bad because the flesh is bad, whereas the spirit is good. Francis rejected this. It was not in the spirit of the Gospel that led him in all things.

Stephen was not finished. He also told them of Brother Philip who had asked that those who criticized the Poor Ladies of San Damiano be excommunicated. This, too, was against what Francis taught the brothers: that they were not to seek privileges of the Holy See or the hierarchy. But what angered him most was that one of the brothers was interfering with and trying to control Lady Clare and the Poor Ladies.

He knew he had to return immediately to Italy before this cancer penetrated the very bones of the brotherhood. Now there was an even harder battle ahead than that of Damietta. The brotherhood was fighting for its life.

Despondent but determined, he summoned Brother Elias, the minister of the Syrian Province and Brother Caesar, also from the Syrian Province, to join Brother Peter and Brother Stephen and Francis himself onboard a Venetian galley returning home. (He wondered if there was any significance to the fact that there were five of them, like the five martyrs he had just learned of.) Francis considered Peter his most trusted vicar, and he recognized in Elias a great talent for organization and leadership, a persuasive man who drew others to the brotherhood, including Caesar, the newly recruited brother from Germany who was a good scribe and biblical scholar. And of course, Brother Stephen the Good, whom Clare had healed of a disease of the soul whereby he had been afflicted by violent outbursts and now was ever calm and even-tempered—until he had to announce the alarming news of what was happening among the brothers in Italy.

The five brothers had had much to talk about and plan on the long journey home, but there was among them the talent and the wisdom to return the brotherhood to its original call from God. Francis was especially grateful for Brother Caesar who would know the Gospels, line and verse, and help them to understand what God's word was saying to them. Together these five would comfort the brothers who were still faithful to their Rule of life; they would censure those who were betraying their obedience to Lady Poverty and the Poor Christ himself.

It had been good having these brothers with him. And Brother Caesar of Speyer did in fact open up the Scriptures for them all along the way. This was deeply consoling to Francis, especially as Brother Stephen revealed to them little by little what was happening in Italy and in particular at the Porziuncola. He told them how there were dissensions everywhere, and how Brother Gregory of Naples, as co-vicar, was advocating that the brothers study and had personally approved the large house of studies to be built in Bologna. He was also asking favors of the Roman Curia in order, he said, to facilitate their preaching and moving about freely in dioceses.

All of this weighed heavily on Francis, and he shared his concerns with these chosen brothers who accompanied him on the journey home. Once when Francis expressed doubts whether or not the Order could survive what he considered the betrayal of the two vicars and their followers, Brother Caesar reminded him that the Order was not his, not Francis's possession, not his vision, but God's. And it had been made manifest to Francis by Christ himself who is the only gate into the sheepfold, no matter what those in authority in the Order might do. He alone was Shepherd, as well. Those brothers who were faithful to him would follow him, as he himself says:

> My sheep hear my voice. I know them, and they follow me. I give them eternal life, and they will never perish. No one will snatch them out of my hand. What my Father has given me is greater than all else, and no one can snatch it out of the Father's hand. The Father and I are one. (John 10:27–30)

"No one will snatch them out of my hand." These words, especially, gave comfort and courage to Francis. For he had seen in a vision at Poggio Bustone, the mountain cave above the Rieti Valley, that the Order would grow into thousands of brothers, but he had forgotten why, until he heard the words of St. John's Gospel. Christ was their Shepherd, not Francis, and he would show Francis and the brothers who wanted to remain faithful to Christ's voice from the cross of San Damiano, what they were to do and how Christ himself would assure that he would remain both their gate and their Shepherd. He would show them how they were to remain faithful to the three openings of the Missal at St. Nicolo, which revealed to them that they were to take nothing for their journey; and that if they were to be Christ's disciples, they were to deny themselves and carry their crosses. Those who heard that voice of Christ, would continue to go in and out of the sheepfold God had made of the Order; those who did not would be snatched away by wolves dressed in sheep's clothing.

But as consoling as these words were, Francis knew that something concrete and practical had to be done if the brothers were going to continue listening to the voice of their true Shepherd. He knew he had to return to Assisi as soon as he could, though the journey would be long from Venice to the Porziuncola, and he was suffering from the pain in his eyes and the heaviness in his heart. So, as in the past when confronted with difficulties or doubts or darkness, he decided that when they arrived in Venice, he would seek out a place of refuge and retreat where he could pray to the Father in the secret closet of his own heart.

His decision to go into solitude made the rest of the journey a happy one, and this time the elements cooperated. It was as though, in deciding to pray instead of react, he had made the decision God wanted; and God calmed the sea and made a smooth, safe passage to Venice.

And so it happened that when they disembarked in Venice, Francis sent the brothers on ahead of him and he rowed out to a small lagoon where on an islet he could enter into the prayer of silence and solitude. But he was so exhausted from the journey and from worry over the brotherhood that when he arrived at the island, he fell into a deep sleep. And while he slept, he dreamed the dream. Always, it seemed, there was the dream when he no longer knew what to do.

. . . .

He saw a small black hen the size of a dove and under its wings
were chicks, too many to fit under the wings of the diminutive

bird. He kept trying to help the chicks, but as soon as he got another one under the wing of the bird, another would be pushed out. And when he awoke, he knew that he was the black hen because of his small stature and dark skin, and the chicks were the brothers now grown too many for him to protect or guide. And the Lord revealed to him that he had not been asleep but resting in God's Spirit, who now inspired him to turn again to the Church, as he had when he and the brothers went to Rome for the approval of the Rule.

. . . .

And so he decided not to go to the Porziuncola directly but to go to the Umbrian town of Orvieto where the papal court resided during August. Then, if it was God's will, he would approach Pope Honorius III and ask for one of the Cardinals as the Protector of the Order and liaison to the Pope himself. He knew he would have to be patient and wait.

And wait he did, perched on the top of the huge yellow rock that Orvieto was built upon rising six hundred feet from the Paglia Valley. And Pope Honorius did grant him an audience and greeted him with, "God bless you, my son."

"And God grant you peace, Holy Father."

"What news do you bring me from the Holy Land?"

Francis could see the Pope's eagerness to know, probably to know how the fighting fared. Instead, he told him of the brothers' endeavor to effect a reconciliation between the Sultan and the Crusader leader, Cardinal Pelagius. Honorius was kind in his response that they were surely following in the footsteps of Christ, but he seemed eager to move on to the business Francis had brought him, overly eager, it seemed, to change the subject of the Sultan Malik al-Kamil and Cardinal Pelagius. Francis wondered how much the Pope knew, but it was not his place to ask. He simply came to the point about the Order's growth and the need for a Cardinal Protector.

Honorius smiled and said that his nephew, Cardinal Ugolino, had already seen that difficulty; and because of his love for the friars, he had asked Honorius to require a novitiate of the incoming brothers, and he had so decreed.

Francis knew that he was walking on thin ice as he proceeded because he suspected that it was probably Cardinal Ugolino who had encouraged Brother Gregory to pursue houses of study for the brothers, houses like those of the Dominicans. He also had heard from Clare that Cardinal Ugolino was trying to impose his own Rule on the Poor Ladies, a Rule more like the Benedictine Rule than Clare and her sisters were comfortable with. He remained silent, praying for words, and then said,

"Yes, Holy Father, that is why we need a Cardinal Protector."

"And do you have anyone in mind, Francis?"

And then (God gave him the insight) he answered,

"Yes, Holy Father, I was thinking of the Bishop of Ostia."

The Holy Father smiled as if he knew what Francis was doing. The Bishop of Ostia was in fact Cardinal Ugolino, the Pope's aforesaid nephew.

"You chose wisely, Brother Francis. I see the hand of God in your choice and in your decision to ask me for a Cardinal Protector. Cardinal Ugolino will, I'm sure, accede to your wish. You could not have a more loyal protector. He loves the brothers and the Poor Ladies of San Damiano and speaks to me often of them. He will do everything in his power to assure the orthodoxy of the Lesser Brothers and the Poor Ladies, and he will work tirelessly to assure that there are continuing vocations to the Poor Brothers and Sisters of Assisi. Go in peace, dear brother, with my blessing. And pray for me that God will guide my decisions regarding the form of life that he gave to you and that was confirmed by my predecessor, Pope Innocent, of happy memory."

And so it was done. It was the best Francis could expect, given the opposing forces among the brothers. And he was confident that Cardinal Ugolino, despite his siding with the leaders of the betrayal during Francis's absence, did have the best interests of the Order in mind. But Francis would not allow any deviance from the Rule as it was approved by Innocent nor any new direction that was against his conscience as the founder of the Order.

Francis knew that God the Holy Spirit was the real founder, and Christ was the Lord who spoke to him from the cross of San Damiano; but it was he that they spoke to and he who had gone in search of God's will when brothers began to join him. If God wanted him to remain as leader of the Order, he would; if not, he would relinquish his authority and return to the brothers as one of those who obey rather than those who give obediences.

And in that he would continue to follow in Jesus's footsteps, he who relinquished worldly power that we might know the true power of the cross.

And that is why in 1221, the year after he returned from the Holy Land, Francis stepped down as General Minister of the Order. He did so during the General Chapter held as usual at the Porziuncola. Brother Peter Catanii became the General Minister.

Francis relinquished power and authority as Jesus had when he became one of us taking the form of a slave and also when he ascended into heaven, leaving the Church the Holy Spirit and the Sacrament of the altar as his presence among us. Jesus himself would henceforth only be seen in the simple elements of bread and wine: the broken bread and wine poured out of the Holy Eucharist. Francis knew that he, too, must become a body broken and consumed by his brothers and blood poured out for them. That was the way of Jesus. That would be his final word to them.

In the meantime he would feed them with words, in prayers, a new Rule of Life, Admonitions, and Letters. And that is what he did.

Cardinal Ugolino had presided at the Chapter, unctuously assuring Francis of how wise his decision was. Now Francis could rest from his labors, he said, and become an icon of their way of life, a mirror of Christ who spoke to him from the cross of San Damiano. He could now let others assume the burdens of the administration of the Order.

And so began his way of the cross, beginning, as with Jesus, with a betrayal. Some of the brothers were already abandoning Lady Poverty for Lady Comfort and Lady Knowledge. Cardinal Ugolino and Brother Elias, among others, both of whom he knew loved him and respected him, assured Francis that they were in no way abandoning Lady Poverty but finding a way to be poor in a world where philosophical and theological heresies were betraying the Creed and the Church, the Bride of Christ. Francis agreed with the problem of the heresies, and it was one of the reasons he did not want the brothers to over-value learning. The Cathari were teaching that because Jesus did not have a real body, there was no Passion, Death, and Resurrection; and therefore we are saved by knowledge of the sayings of Jesus that help us free the good soul from the bad body. Over and over again Francis emphasized that we are saved not by knowledge but by the Passion, Death, and Resurrection of Jesus Christ.

But he did not see how compromising evangelical poverty would help fight heresy and make the brothers more effective in preaching the Gospel. What could he do to counteract the learned arguments of those like Cardinal Ugolino and Brother Elias? He would state directly in the new Rule he was writing that the brothers may not make any claim to learning, but rather strive for that devotion which hears the word of God and immediately goes forth to accomplish what the Lord commands and admonishes them to do. And in all they do, they should let nothing extinguish the spirit of prayer and holy devotion to which everything else should be subservient.

The abuses of the learned friars and other abuses he would counteract directly as the Lord inspired him to do. He wondered how much of what he would put into the Rule Cardinal Ugolino would allow? He prayed that the Church would at least keep the words of Jesus, which he was determined to insert into the Rule. Brother Caesar of Speyer would track down the sources of the words he held in his heart, the words he had memorized from the very beginning, words that gave him spirit and life.

And so emerged the Rule of 1221, which the Holy Father did not confirm because it was more a spiritual document than a canonical Rule that others could live and that the Church could live with. That was the first fall on the way to Calvary. The second fall was the suffering and troubles he encountered in drafting the new Rule of 1223—twelve short chapters edited by Cardinal Ugolino's legal mind and approved by Pope Honorius III. While he was praying and working on this Rule at the hermitage of Fonte Colombo near Rieti, the brothers sent a delegation to him to tell him they were afraid they would not be able to live this new Rule. His only defense was that they could live this Rule because Christ himself was dictating it to him.

They liked the word "dictating," because he was evidently listening as well as writing his own prejudices about what the Order should be. What they balked at was that it was Christ who was dictating. But they soon left when he would not reveal to them what he was putting into the Rule, telling them that they had to trust in Christ and in the Holy Spirit, the true General Minister of the Order.

The third fall was the ongoing deterioration of his health, the cauterization of his eyes by a physician in Rieti which did not arrest the rapid loss of his sight, and, worst of all, the ongoing changes in the Order that countered the early years of the first brothers, the honeymoon of their espousal to Lady Poverty.

But then something surprising happened to lift the hearts of the brothers who were with him in Rieti. Even now, so many years after their marriage to Lady Poverty, a child was born of their union. It took place on Christmas Eve at Greccio in the year of Our Lord, 1223. Greccio: their small cave of a hermitage on the hillside opposite the mountain village of Greccio in the Rieti Valley, the navel of Italy and of the world. It was there that Christ, the baby Jesus, was born again—an inestimable gift to the brothers who had remained faithful to Lady Poverty. Of their chaste union was born Christ the Lord.

Some of the brothers had been insisting that the Order could not be reborn into the image of what it was at the beginning. They could not continue to live on visions and dreams; the infancy of the Order was just that—infancy— and now they must live on stronger food than the milk of babies.

And then came Greccio, and the Infant was born again, and Francis took him in his arms. And this is how it was.

It started simply. He wanted to celebrate Christmas in a new way by recreating the stable of Bethlehem. He would have a real ox and ass there, and they would celebrate Mass outside the cave with a bare rock for an altar. Francis, who was a deacon, would read the Gospel and preach to the brothers and the townspeople of Greccio whom the brothers would invite to midnight Mass.

He asked a local nobleman, John of Velita, a devout man devoted to the brothers, to make the preparations. And all went as planned. In the heart of night the townspeople crossed from Greccio to the hermitage carrying lighted candles and singing Christmas songs. They were amazed at the scene before them, the live Christmas crib that made them see the poverty and humility of God.

So excited was Francis that when he preached, he could not say *Bethlehem* without bleating like a lamb when he pronounced the word, "Betlemme." And when the people looked curiously at him, he told them that he had become a lamb and they should, too, in order to honor this Little Lamb of God born to them this night. There was no baby lying on the straw because Francis knew that the one to be born in the Mass was he who was born in Bethlehem.

But when he finished preaching, he turned to the crèche and saw a little baby lying on the stone altar, the Little Word of God made flesh; and he took it in his arms. He didn't know if the people saw what he held, but they would understand the pantomime, the gesture of reaching down to the altar and lifting something tenderly to his heart.

It was the dearest of Christmases and lifted Francis's heart from the depths to which it had fallen. Like the hermitage of Greccio itself, his faith, that had been clinging desperately to the side of the mountain, let go. And the hermitage did not plummet to the valley below, nor did his faith. It was lifted up with the baby he lifted in his arms.

The people remained after the Mass and prayed in the makeshift stable. They asked if they could have some of the straw strewn over the dirt floor for the animals. And when they took it home, Francis heard that animals were healed in eating a portion of the hay, and women undergoing a difficult birth happily and safely delivered their babies. And Francis gave thanks and praised God that indeed this was a new birth of Christ, the Baby and Little Lamb of God.

THE YEAR OF OUR LORD 1224

Lovescape

And now it was La Verna, one year after the miracle of
Greccio, and Brother Leo was saying Mass. No baby appeared
on the simple altar, no miracle of straw, but the presence of
Jesus was tangible to Francis, Jesus at the Last Supper, Jesus
embracing him again in the breaking of the bread and in the
pouring out of his blood like a rich and mature wine. In his
blindness he could see the altar and Brother Leo only dimly,
but he could see to see what was happening inside the blur.

. . . .

"Oh Brother Leo!" How many times he had said these words!
How many years he'd added, "Write down this, Brother Leo."
And Leo unquestioningly wrote down Francis's poor words,
enriching them and blessing them with his prayers, Leo, his
brother, his priest, his scribe.

He knew Leo would be good for the brotherhood the very first
time he saw him. His feet gave him away. They were small and
tight and tough skinned. He was a priest and therefore unused
to going without shoes. But the potential was there. Once he
began to walk barefoot in the footsteps of Jesus those feet would

toughen even more. He had the feet of a poor begging brother. He would make it on the road. And so he had, Leo with the small, compact feet, with the head that seemed too big for his feet and gave him that sort of wobbly look that was only an illusion. As soon as he began to walk, those scrubby little feet took over; and big head or not, they were in charge.

. . . .

And now here they were together again at La Verna, their sacred mountain, preparing for the Feast of St. Michael the Archangel, and Leo was praying the Mass of the Exaltation of the Holy Cross, his feet planted firmly on the rocky ground. He raised his heart to Leo's voice in the Introit's perfect articulation: *"Nos autem gloriari opportet in cruce Domini Nostri Jesu Christi: in quo est salus, vita et resurrectio nostra: per quem salvati et liberati sumus.* We however should glory in the cross of Our Lord Jesus Christ in whom is our salvation, life and resurrection through which we are saved and made free."

The wind began to whistle and whine through the pine trees as Brother Leo intoned, *"Kyrie eleison, Christe eleison, Kyrie eleison."* That cry, like that of the pines, for mercy. Lord, be merciful to me, a sinner. And sinner he had been and was, but lately he seemed to remember more the blessings of Jesus.

. . . .

Jesus. How often in turning to him, Francis had seen what he must do: how Jesus was the Shepherd, but also the Gate of the sheepfold; and he was also the Lamb who takes away the sins of the world. When he is the Shepherd, we are the lambs; when he is the Gate, we enter through him into the Father; when he is the Lamb, he is one of us being led by the Father's will.

Whenever Francis listened to Brother Leo or Brother Sylvester, or one of the other brother priests intone the "Agnus Dei," "Lamb of God who take away the sins of the world, have mercy on us," he would think of Lamb, Gate, Shepherd. Jesus: the Lamb who died that we might live, the Shepherd who leads us into the kingdom of the Father through the Gate, which is Christ himself and the very altar of the Mass upon which the Passion, Death, and Resurrection of Christ is re-enacted. Everything, the whole of God's will for the brothers was incarnated in the Mass. The Mass was their way of life.

It began with the entrance antiphon that leads into the sheepfold where resides the Shepherd and the Lamb of sacrifice. And the entrance itself is the sign of the cross, for in no other sign will we be saved.

This was Francis's own experience when God began to call him. It began with Entrance Antiphons of his dreams which in turn led him to embrace the cross of conversion, of the need for change in his life. And with the call to conversion came the awareness of his sins and the need for God's mercy and forgiveness; *Kyrie eleison, Christe eleison, Kyrie eleison:* Lord, have mercy, Christ have mercy, Lord have mercy.

Then, knowing God's mercy, so freely, generously given, his whole life broke into song, Gloria in excelsis Deo. Glory to God in the highest, for that alone brings peace to God's people on earth. That was what had brought peace between Francis and Sultan Malik al-Kamil, their mutual adoration of God, referring all glory to God in the highest.

For the Church and for Francis this God is "Lord God, heavenly King, almighty God and Father." God is the King, who in Jesus and through him, is revealed as our Father for whose glory we must worship, thank, and praise him.

In the first part of the Mass was summed up the whole beginning of the brothers' vocation: the call to conversion, the recognition of one's need for God's mercy, the giving of glory to God alone. Then followed the rest of the "Gloria" of the Mass—most of it centered on the Lord, Jesus Christ, who is Son of the Father, Lord God, Lamb of God who takes away the sins of the world. We ask him to have mercy on us, for he is seated at the right hand of the Father to receive our prayer. For Jesus Christ alone is the Holy One, the Lord, the Most High, who dwells with the Holy Spirit, in the glory of God the Father.

For Francis all that the brothers needed to know in order to pray was contained in the words of the "Gloria" of the Mass. But in order to live their lives informed by the Mass itself, they needed the readings of the Mass. They needed to hear God's word proclaimed to them so that they might know God's story in which was revealed God's will for them: how they might make of their whole life an ascent to the Most High God, Jesus Christ, who descended to us that we might ascend with him, we the sheep of his sheepfold.

And so now here on La Verna he listened intently and prayerfully to the readings for the Feast of the Exaltation of the Holy

Cross. The first reading was from the book of Numbers and told about how seraph serpents bit the people in the desert, and so Moses prayed to God for the people, and God told him to make and lift up on a pole a bronze serpent so that the people could look upon it and be healed of their snake bites. And the people who were bitten did as God asked, and they recovered.

Francis wondered about the seraph serpents. Was the serpent in the Garden of Eden one of these? Was its bite the sting of sin? The bronze serpent on the pole reminded him of Jesus on the cross. But how could he be shown to us as a serpent? It was a bit confusing until Brother Leo began to explain what Brother Caesar had told them after Mass one day. The Church had given us this reading on the Feast of the Exaltation of the Holy Cross because just as the Israelites looked upon the bronze serpent and were healed of the deadly bite of the seraph serpents, so we must look upon Jesus lifted up on the cross if we are to be healed of the deadly poison of Satan, the serpent of the Garden of Eden.

That Francis could understand. For that is what he tried to do and taught his friars to do: Keep your eyes fixed on the Lord Jesus Christ. For the cross, too, was a part of the glory of the Most High.

And what Leo said and Caesar said was confirmed by St. John's Gospel of this glorious Feast when Jesus says, "And just as Moses lifted up the serpent in the wilderness, so must the Son of Man be lifted up, that whoever believes in him may have eternal life" (John 3:14–15). How often in his life after his conversion had the Gospel explained one or another of the readings to him!

It was the second reading of this Feast, however, that moved him the most: St. Paul's Letter to the Philippians wherein Paul defines for the brothers what is the model of what it means to be a poor brother of penance following in the footsteps of him

> who, though he was in the form of God,
> did not regard equality with God
> as something to be exploited,
> but emptied himself,
> taking the form of a slave
> being born in human likeness.
> And being found in human form,
> he humbled himself
> and became obedient to the point of death—
> even death on a cross. (2:6–8)

These words of St. Paul were the very core of why they chose to be poor, chaste, and obedient. They were who they were because they were trying to follow in the footsteps of Christ whose self-emptying was his real glory and whose invitation to us was to make the same self-emptying journey with him.

If we did, we would also reign with him, but more importantly, we would show our love for him. To walk the way of the Shepherd, the Gate, and the Lamb was to relinquish being Shepherd and Gate to become the Lamb of Sacrifice. Nor could the Christ relinquish being Shepherd and Gate, except by becoming human and thereby revealing his hidden Divinity that he could not relinquish completely, for it was who he was. He merely set aside the power and the glory to embrace fully the poverty and helplessness of the human being.

What sacrifice was here—that God himself actually felt human suffering, took it upon himself; and because he was also God, he felt the cumulative suffering of all humanity for all time. There could be no greater suffering than his. And he did it all out of infinite love for us. To share, then, in that suffering and death in our own small way was to join Jesus in loving the Father and in loving other human beings.

That was what it meant to be Shepherd, namely, to become Lamb, as well, become helpless as a Lamb led to slaughter because he chose to do so.

How could anyone not respond to such love! How could we, too, not lay down our lives out of love for him who laid down his life for love of us? In that is rising; in that is our resurrection with Christ.

. . . .

Francis was lost in these thoughts, as he often was of late, when he was shaken out of his reverie by Brother Leo's beautiful chanting of the words of the Preface of the Holy Cross. Francis was transfixed by the words, *"Qui salutem humani generis in ligno crucis constituisti: ut unde mors oriebatur, inde vita resurgeret: et qui in ligno vincebat, in ligno quoque vinceretur."* ("You decreed that the salvation of the human race be on the wood of the cross: so that where life was lost, life would rise again: the tree of defeat became also the tree of victory.")

. . . .

The tree of the cross: "Foolishness to those who are perishing... but to those who are called.... Christ the power of God and the wisdom of God" (see 1 Corinthians 1:18, 21). He could see the tree and upon it him whom he loved with all his heart, Jesus Christ, the Son of God. Jesus's powerlessness—as the world defines power—was the vocation of the brothers: the powerlessness of the Babe of Greccio, the powerlessness of the Crucified Christ of La Verna—both of them freely chosen by the King who humbled himself to the point of being like us in the human powerlessness to be born on our own and to die on our own. All was dependent on the will of the Father. It was the brothers' vocation to live in a way that imitates the humility of God.

Francis felt deeply his own powerlessness. His body was beginning to fail him. Many of the brothers were beyond his reach, and his hold on the vision of God's revelation to him seemed to be slipping beyond his grasp.

But as the Mass continued, it became clear that like Christ in the Garden of Gethsemane, he must choose to let go of his own will and say with Jesus, "Not my will but your will be done" (see Matthew 26:39). Already at the Preface of the Mass he had felt himself surrendering in a way he had not done this completely. And during the Canon of the Mass he could feel something like an angel leading him to the Consecration.

He felt the bread and wine changing; he felt the pain which that change cost Jesus on the cross: the broken body, the blood flowing out. And when Brother Leo placed the host upon his tongue, it was as if his very self was subsumed into Christ rather than as before when Holy Communion was as if Francis were taking Christ into himself and Christ permeated his whole body as food is absorbed in the body. Now it was he who was being consumed by Christ and entering him completely, his own sense of himself lost in the Beloved.

Brother Masseo had to lead him back to the other brothers gathered around the altar. And even then he was scarcely aware of Masseo and the other brothers. He no longer was aware of now or movement or the passage of time.

. . . .

Everyone but Leo was gone when he awoke. The trees of the forest surrounded him, all of them crosses on which hung the Savior of the World.

He asked Brother Leo to stand guard, as he wanted now to enter into prayer and solitude. Then he crossed over a makeshift bridge to his place of hermitage far enough away that he could hear Brother Leo only if he hollered across the ravine to Francis. And he rested in the Mass he still carried within him. He continued to be absorbed into Christ.

THE YEAR OF OUR LORD 1224

Transfiguration

None of the brothers knew the whole story of what happened next, and Francis did not speak of it. He hid the secret, and the brothers dared not surmise what had transpired between Francis and the Blessed Savior. Only Brother Leo knew something, however little, of what happened that day on Mount La Verna.

Brother Leo noticed something happening, some change, that morning as he was chanting the Holy Mass and began to intone the Preface. It was as though his Father Francis then began to be inside the very words of the Preface. And at the time of the Consecration Father Francis seemed somehow transported, almost as if he was in an ecstatic state. And when he gave him the Holy Eucharist, the light from within Francis filled Leo with such sweetness of soul as he'd never experienced before. But Father Francis himself was not able to return to his place without Brother Masseo taking his arm.

Now it begins, Leo thought, his holy father's own inner Mass of the Exaltation of the Holy Cross. He could see it in his face and movements.

After Mass Francis asked him to walk with him to the log bridge that led to his place of prayer in the woods. He walked as if in a trance with a slow, dreamlike pace, an abstracted expression on his face. And when they came to the log bridge, Francis wanted to go on alone. He said, "I want to be alone with Jesus."

Then, as he had done before, Francis asked Leo to withdraw some distance from him and to keep calling out until he no longer returned Leo's salutations. Leo was to stay in that place and come to Francis only in the evenings to pray matins with him.

But that very night of the Feast of the Holy Cross when Leo drew near the log that served as a bridge over a deep chasm that separated him from Francis and called out, *"Domine, labia mea aperies,"* "Lord, open my lips," there was no answer. He knew he should have gone back to his place when Francis did not answer, as he had been instructed to do. But he feared that something might be wrong. Francis was in such a weakened state when he walked to the bridge that morning and then seemed to almost glide when he'd crossed over the chasm and neared his place of hermitage. Leo actually wondered if Francis had passed over into eternity, so different was his pace and carriage once he had crossed over the chasm. He began to move as into another dimension.

Was Leo—like one of the Apostles on Mount Tabor—about to

witness a vision that he would not have eyes to see? Would he hear what he could not see? Thinking these thoughts, Leo now disobeyed Father Francis and dared to cross over the chasm even though Francis had told him not to unless he was summoned. He walked stealthily, quietly, to Francis's place in the woods. But he could see in the bright moonlight that Francis was not there. So, thinking he must have wandered off, or perhaps something untoward may have happened to him somewhere in the woods, Leo began to search for him by the light of the moon. He did not call out lest he disturb Francis should he only be lost in prayer.

Before long he began to hear his holy father's voice and quietly moved in that direction until he saw him bathed in moonlight, kneeling on the ground and saying aloud with almost painful ardor of spirit, "Who are you, dearest God? And what am I, your vilest little worm and useless little servant?" He repeated these words over and over again like a lover's mournful refrain.

Leo stood motionless and tense fearing Francis might sense his presence and interrupt his prayer. He kept his eyes fixed on the heavens where Father Francis gazed with rapt attention and prayed with such anguish of spirit. Leo prayed with him in his heart.

Then, as if in answer to their combined prayer, a bright and beautiful tongue of fire appeared in the sky and descended to Francis and rested on his head, and a voice began to speak to him. Francis then replied as Leo cautiously withdrew. Leo did not want to hear what was not his to hear.

And when there was no longer any possibility that he might hear Francis or Francis hear him, Leo turned and stood still to see what he could see. Within minutes he saw Francis hold out his hand three times to the flame now hovering before him.

Finally, after the flame and Francis had remained suspended for what seemed a long time, the flame moved slowly into the sky and disappeared.

Consoled, then, and filled with an indescribable joy, Leo began to steal away toward the log bridge. But as he carefully moved through the underbrush, he stumbled and landed on some dead leaves and twigs. The voice of Francis startled him where he lay holding his breath.

"Whoever you are, I command you in the name of Our Lord, Jesus Christ, to stay where you are. Do not move from that spot!"

Leo rose and stood trembling, afraid that Father Francis would be angry and disappointed and berate him for his idle curiosity. He was terrified that his father Francis would now no longer trust him or confide in him or consider him his faithful friend. He knew Francis was the greatest of saints and did not know how he would live without his friendship.

He stood holding his breath as Francis approached stumbling from time to time in his blindness. Leo wanted to rush up to him and help him, but he couldn't move in his fear of frightening or upsetting Father Francis by once again being disobedient to the command to stay where he was.

At last Francis drew near and asked, "Who are you?"

"Father Francis, it is I, Brother Leo."

"Leo? But why did you come here, Little Brother Lamb?"

Leo almost fainted when he heard the tenderness in Francis's voice and when he called him "Little Brother Lamb"—him, Leo, the lion.

"Did I not warn you many times not to follow me around watching me? And tell me, under holy obedience, Little Lamb, did you hear or see anything?"

Leo's heart leaped into his throat. "Under holy obedience." He had to tell his father Francis how he had in fact betrayed his trust.

"Father Francis, please forgive me. I saw you on your knees, and I heard you praying and saying over and over, 'Who are you, my dearest God, and what am I, your vilest worm and useless little servant?'

His heart sank as he continued headlong into his confession: "And then I saw a flame of fire come down from heaven and seem to talk with you, and you replied. But I could not hear. And then you held out your hand to the flame three times."

He then fell to his knees before Francis; and with tears running down his cheeks, he confessed his sin of disobedience and begged again for forgiveness from Francis, who smiling, put his hand upon Leo's head and blessed him saying, "Oh, Brother Leo, Little Lamb, there is nothing to forgive. What you did you did out of love for me—and curiosity, too, and the desire to know. You must understand, dear brother, that what God wants us to know God will show us, provided it is for our salvation. So, what you should ever be curious to know is God and all God's ways, dear brother, not me and God's ways with me; for I, like you, am but a poor sinner and as nothing compared to Jesus Christ, the true Lamb and Shepherd of our souls. Now, Little Lamb, rise up in joy and retire to the consolation of Christ who loves you with an everlasting love."

Leo was overcome that Father Francis should say so much to make him feel forgiven and loved. He wanted to rise immediately and leave Francis to his solitude, but something held him back, some need to preserve for all the brothers what had happened here, and so he fool heartedly pressed on as if he had not heard his father's words.

"Dear father, thank you. I am leaving now; but, please forgive me, before I do, does our loving Savior have something to say to all the brothers to console them—some word, perhaps, of what he said to you and you said to him when you reached out your hand three times?"

There was a long, not uncomfortable pause. And then Francis said quite simply that what he was about to say was for Leo's ears only because Leo was simple and without guile, and he must not tell the brothers till after Francis had died lest the brothers think their father holier than he was and thereby concentrate on him rather than on the marvelous works of God.

He told Leo then of how the day before when he was in the place of prayer and solitude an angel had appeared to him with this message from God: "I encourage and urge you to prepare to receive with all patience what God will to do in you." And Brother Francis answered the angel: "I am prepared to endure patiently whatever my Lord wants to do in me." (Leo thought of our Blessed Mother Mary saying to the Archangel Gabriel, "Be it done to me according to your will.")

"Then the angel departed. But there is more, Brother Leo. This morning after Mass when I returned to the place of prayer in the woods, I was moved by God's grace to turn to the east and fall to my knees, and these words poured from my mouth all in a steady stream sweet as honey. They came from within, almost as if the Lord I had received in the holy Mass was speaking the very words I was speaking.

"And these are the words my overflowing heart spoke to the east where the sun was just beginning to light the blessed sky of La Verna: 'My Lord Jesus Christ, I pray that you grant me two graces before I die: that during my life I may feel in my soul and body, as much as my poor self can, the pain which you, dear Jesus, patiently endured in the hour of your most bitter Passion. And secondly, that I may feel in my heart, as much as possible for one so poor as I, that excess of love which inflamed you, the Son of God, to willingly endure such suffering for sinners like me.'"

Then Father Francis blessed Leo and asked him to return to his place of prayer which Leo did all willingly, not turning back to see what further wonders God might work in Francis. And what wonders they were, as he was to learn later.

It is now two years since Leo and Francis left Brothers
Masseo and Angelo on the holy mountain and bade farewell
to them and to Brother Sylvester, and Brother Illuminato
before descending the mountain, La Verna. Francis rode on a
donkey because he was not able then to walk without excru-
ciating pain the source of which Leo would tell only when
Francis was dying.

When they finally returned to Assisi, Francs wanted to go
first to San Damiano where Clare and the other Poor Ladies
dwelled. And there he asked that a simple dwelling of sticks
and branches be made where he could lie down and rest. He
could see virtually nothing by then, and the sun by day and
candle by night caused his eyes to bleed.

He lay thus in darkness with field mice, which the brothers
could not contain, running over his poor, emaciated body.
His spirit, too, was low because some of the brothers were
still constructing buildings to dwell in, and, in some cases,
to study in.

For over fifty days he lay there while Leo ministered to
him and changed the bandages that contained the blood
outpoured for the brothers and for all the people of God.
And it was there, during those long days and nights, whenever he had strength enough to speak, that Francis revealed
to Leo the mystery of La Verna.

As he spoke, sometimes haltingly and at other times all in
a flow, Leo could see again La Verna and hear the birds and
feel the wind rushing through the trees and whining in the
huge rocks hanging precariously over the ravine—rocks that

Francis told him were split apart at the hour when Christ died upon the cross. Blessed be Christ's Holy Name!

Francis would usually talk to Leo for a short time after Leo had dressed the wounds of the Blessed Crucified Jesus. Piecing it all together from the fragments of Francis's halting account, this is the story told simply and as well as Leo could remember.

After he left his holy father Francis on that fateful night of the Feast of the Exaltation of the Holy Cross, as Francis told Leo later with much fervor of heart and many tears, he began to contemplate the sacred Passion and Death of his Savior. And so intense was the love that filled his heart as he meditated upon Jesus on the cross, that it seemed to him the very wounds he contemplated in Jesus were breaking forth from within his own body.

While he was lost thus in contemplation, his eyes closed, his face turned toward the eastern sky, he heard a beating of wings. And opening his eyes, he saw a flaming Seraph hovering in the sky and beginning to move toward him. The angel had six wings, two elevated above him, two outstretched in flight, and two covering his whole body. And as the Seraph drew nearer, the two wings covering his body suddenly opened revealing the body of a man, and the man was the crucified Jesus Christ. Francis trembled in awe and was filled with compassion for the suffering Son of Man, but with joy, too, when he saw the exquisite look of love on the face of Jesus.

The light emanating from the Seraph illumined the whole mountain and lit up the sky as if the sun had already risen. And the light was pulsating like the sun itself.

Father Francis felt then a love so intense that he thought he would not be able to endure it. And when he thought he might faint of love, a voice, the same voice he'd heard speak to him from the San Damiano cross years before, spoke to him from the Seraph-man hovering above him. It told him of secret things Father Francis never shared completely with anyone, saying he was afraid to make public the secrets of God.

But Brother Illuminato, who'd been with him when he went to the court of the Sultan and who was present once when Francis was recounting to him and Leo something of what happened, said, "Dear Brother Francis, isn't it true that in the past God has shown you his divine mysteries not just for you to know but for the good of others? So, wouldn't you be guilty of hiding Christ's light under a bushel basket if you refuse to tell us what might be for the good of many?"

At that Francis again began to recount with halting awe-filled words the vision Leo later imparted, adding that Christ had told him some things that he could not tell anyone as long as he lived, except for one message: "I have given you the stigmata which are the emblems of my Passion so that you might be my standard-bearer."

Francis then added that after a long, intimate conversation between Jesus and him, the vision disappeared leaving a flaming sword of divine love in his heart. He began to feel intense pain as though a red hot poker had been thrust into his hands and feet and side. And when he looked at his body, still illumined by the light of the departed Seraph, he saw nails beginning to emerge from his flesh. His hands and feet were pierced with nails whose heads were round and black and protruded from the palms of his hands and the upper part of his feet. The points of the nails emerged from the backs of his hands and the soles of his feet and seemed bent and hammered into a small ring one could almost put one's finger through. In his side was an open, bleeding wound.

His two prayers had been answered. He began to praise God, feeling in his heart an almost unbearable love of Jesus Christ crucified. He retired to the woods in prayer for long hours and days and seemed to be living in the Resurrection. And that was all.

Leo reflected that the Risen Lord, the Most High, as Father Francis called him, is present under the appearance of the bread and wine of the Mass. There, Francis had told them, Jesus is present as the Most Low, who, in the words of Francis's First Admonition to the brothers, "humbles himself just as he did when he came from his heavenly throne into the Virgin's womb; everyday he comes to us and lets us see him in abjection when he descends from the bosom of the Father into the hands of the priest at the altar. He shows himself to us in this sacred bread just as he once appeared to his Apostles in real flesh. With their own eyes they saw only his flesh, but they believed that he was God because they contemplated him with the eyes of the spirit. We, too, with our own eyes see only bread and wine, but we must see further and believe that his is the most holy Body and Blood, living and true. In this way our Lord remains continually with his followers as he promised: 'Behold, I am with you all days, even unto the consummation of the world.'"

Leo was himself aware of these words when he celebrated Mass on Mount La Verna that precious day when the Risen Lord had entered into Father Francis in the form of bread and wine and Francis became thereby a living image of who it was he had received. What seemed to come to him from without in the form of a burning Seraphic Angel, came first from within him in the form of Father Francis's complete transformation into the Most High he had received into himself as the Most Low.

What great mystery is here: that the Risen Christ is the Crucified Christ, and the Crucified Christ is the Risen Christ. And that is what Francis had become for the brothers even before he was signed with the sacred stigmata: a crucified image of the Risen Christ. How deep and mysterious it is and how mixed were the brothers' feelings about it. They wanted to rejoice that Christ was among them in Francis, and at the same time they wanted to weep that Christ continued to suffer in Francis.

When Jesus told Francis that he was to be Christ's standard-bearer, Leo added in his own mind: "*Yes, and he is a standard-bearer of us, as well; for we are all called to be standard-bearers of the crucified Risen Christ. The human and the divine together; death and rising made real in all through the real flesh and blood of God in the Holy Eucharist."*

But enough of such complicated thinking. No wonder Leo's head was bigger than his feet. He must remember his stumbling lamb's feet and how often he had not walked the thoughts that elevated him higher than he really was.

He was, after all, the one who had begun to feel sorry for himself on La Verna because of fears and temptations that plagued him while Father Francis prayed devoutly in contemplation of his crucified Lord. He was the one who longed secretly to have some word of comfort from Francis that was just for him. He was the one who didn't know that Francis would know what he was thinking. He was the one Francis summoned and chided gently for being afraid to disturb his solitude.

"Brother Leo, Little Lamb, you mustn't ever hesitate to come to me, even in my solitude, if you truly need me—you especially, for you have always been there for me in every need. You are the one who inspired me to write in the Rule that we are to confidently make known our need to our brother— as you had allowed me to do—that he might know what we need and minister to us, and that every brother must care for his brother as a mother cares for her son."

Then Francis asked for a scrap of parchment such as Leo often used to write down the things Francis asked him to transcribe. And in his own hand Francis wrote some new praises of God which had come to him in prayer during the days after the vision of the Seraph Angel. Francis sounded the words as he wrote them down.

You are holy, Lord,
God alone, who works marvels.
You are strong and grand and Most High.
You are the All-Powerful, Holy Father,
King of heaven and earth.
You are three and one, Lord God of gods.
You are the good, every good, the highest good.
the Lord God, living and true.
You are love, charity, wisdom, humility, patience.
You are beauty, safety, and rest.
You are joy and gladness.
You are our hope and our justice and our temperance.
You are all our treasure overflowing.
You are beauty and meekness.
You are our protector, our guardian and our defender.
You are strength and refreshment.
You are our hope, our faith, our charity.
You are all our sweetness.
You are our eternal great and wondrous Lord,
God all-powerful, merciful Savior.

Then turning the paper over, Francis penned these words, again sounding them as he wrote:

May God bless you and keep you,
Show his face and be merciful to you,
Turn his face toward you and give you peace.

He then sketched a crude head and drew the letter tau issuing from the mouth of the head. And he wrote these additional words with the tau cross intersecting Leo's name: "God bless you, Brother Leo."

When Leo saw that Francis had signed him with the tau, the sign of the elect, he was moved to tears. Then Francis handed the paper to him and said, "Take this, Little Sheep, and keep it with you as long as you live." Leo kissed it reverently, and all his inner doubt and turmoil seemed as nothing. He folded the paper carefully and put it inside his habit next to his heart. He keep it to the end of his life—not as a possession, but as Francis's words made real on paper as God's words are made real in bread and wine.

From the hour of the sacred stigmata Brother Leo became the intimate whom Father Francis chose to bandage and dress his wounds, some weeks as many times as once a day, except from Thursday evening till Saturday morning; for on those days of Christ's own Passion Francis did not want his own pain to be alleviated by any salve or cleansing.

Sometimes when Leo changed the dressings, Father Francis would be in so much pain that he would place his hand on Leo's chest over his heart, and Leo's heart would burn with such warmth and exquisite love of God as he had never felt. How marvelous are the works and love of God! Even to Leo with his lion's head and tiny lamb's feet that Father Francis took so much joy in.

There were days during his time of great suffering that Leo would walk into his father's cell in the morning, and Francis would start to bleat like a lamb instead of greeting him with his usual, "The Lord give you peace, dear Brother

Leo." And they would both smile and Leo would roar like a lion then pad around the cell stumbling into things like a lamb. It always seemed to lighten both their hearts, this silly banter that Francis's unrelieved suffering seemed to make possible again, a kind of joy that was not in spite of, but because of the pain.

On days like that Francis would bless Leo when he left, as usual, but add something like, "Now hurry back to the sheep-fold and watch out for the wolves, especially those in sheep's skins." And Francis would wink and fall back exhausted onto the straw.

Toward the end of the time when Francis lay in darkness and pain at San Damiano, he sensed that he would soon begin to sing again, but about what he did not know, nor did Leo or the other brothers.

Jesus now inhabited his waking hours more than ever. He told Leo that in his pain, especially, Jesus seemed like someone inside him struggling to be born anew in order to say something further to the brothers and all whose lives they touched. It was as if the pain he experienced was a kind of childbirth, and the child was Jesus and Francis at the same time. Sometimes his pain and weakness were so great that it seemed he could no longer go on, that whatever word was struggling to be born would kill him in its coming to birth.

One day when the pain was especially intense, he was once again visited by the voice he had grown familiar with, the voice he had first heard at this same San Damiano at the beginning of his conversion.

Francis told the brothers with tears in his eyes that shone at the same time with joy that the voice had said to him:

"Brother Francis, if you were now given the immense and precious treasure of the whole earth changing into pure gold, pebbles turning to precious stones, and rivers changing to perfume, would you not consider the earth and pebbles and rivers as nothing compared to such a transformation?"

He told the brothers afterward that he knew what the voice was saying: This was the kingdom, the new heaven and the new earth. He could see it all in his mind: a new Eden that his Lord was now about to assure him was his, and he was to embrace it as compensation for his present suffering.

"Yes, Lord," Father Francis answered. "It would be a great, precious, and inestimable treasure beyond anything that one could love and desire. It is the treasure I have looked for from the moment I began to seek you in the cave on Mount Subasio."

And then he fell into a deep sleep.

The next morning he rose as if made anew. The pain was still there and the blindness, but everything seemed bathed in the light of God's promise. And when Leo came into his cell, he could not restrain his joy:

Oh, Brother Leo, I now rejoice in my trials and infirmities and seek my consolation in the Lord, giving thanks to the Father; the Son, our Lord Jesus Christ, and the Holy Spirit. For God in his mercy has condescended to assure me, his poor unworthy

servant, that while still living on this earth, I will
share his kingdom. And indeed, Little Lamb, the
earth and all that is in it, including me, this suffering,
weak man lying here, has somehow been turned into
a radiant gift of God. And I cannot contain myself,
dearest Leo. I must sing again—for me and for you
and for all human beings and all creatures.

And he began to sing full-throated and sweetly. Leo
scratched the words down as quickly as he could, knowing
that this could be Francis's final song. And this is what
Francis sang:

Most High, all-powerful, Good Lord,
yours is the praise,
the glory and the honor
and every blessing.
To you alone, Most High, do they belong,
and no one is worthy
to speak your name.
Praised be you, my Lord, with all your creatures,
especially Sir Brother Sun who makes
day and enlightens us through you.
And he is lovely, shining with great splendor
for he heralds you, Most High.
Praised be you, my Lord, through Sister Moon and
    Stars;
in heaven you have formed them
lightsome and precious and fair.

Praised be you, my Lord, through Brother Wind,
and through air and cloud
and calm and every weather
through which you sustain your creatures.
Praised be you, my Lord, through Sister Water,
so very useful and humble
and precious and chaste.
Praised be you, my Lord, through Brother Fire,
through whom you illumine our night.
And he is handsome and merry,
robust and strong.
Praised be you, my Lord, for our sister Mother
  Earth
in her sovereignty she nourishes us,
bringing forth all kinds of fruits
with colored flowers and herbs.

What combinations were here! Earth, water, wind, and fire were now our brothers and sisters; and Francis praised God through them and with them.

In these holy words the Incarnation of God in Jesus Christ somehow dwelled. Because Jesus walked the earth, it became our sister charged with fruitfulness; because Jesus went down into the Jordan River and was baptized by John and because he said he was living water, then our Sister Water is pure and chaste; because Jesus breathed the air and breathed out his spirit when he died, Brother Wind is the sustaining breath of God, breathing all things; because Jesus said he came to

bring fire upon the earth, then Brother Fire is now a transforming fire that lights up the darkness of our lives and puri-
fies our love.

There was that and so much more that Leo didn't understand but felt deep in his heart whenever he sang "The
Canticle of the Creatures."

But Francis was not finished singing. For when a dispute
arose between the Bishop and the mayor of Assisi, he sang
another stanza and added it to the Canticle. He asked
Brother Pacifico, who had been a famous troubadour in the
world, to sing it before the Bishop and the mayor. While
Pacifico sang, Francis would pray, and they would be recon-
ciled. And so they were with this simple stanza:

> Praised be you, my Lord, for those who forgive
> for love of your love and
> who bear sickness and trial.
> Blessed are those who endure in peace,
> for by you, Most High,
> they will be crowned.

Father Francis knew, it seems, the inner power God invested
in the words that sprang up spontaneously from his gratitude
for the assurance of God's kingdom.

Then when Father Francis came to die, he sang the final
stanzas of his Canticle, knowing full well the words would
give him hope and courage to make the passage into the
kingdom that already dwelled within him, a mirror of the
kingdom he was about to return to.

Praised be you, my Lord, through our Sister
Bodily Death from whom
no one living can escape.
Woe to those who die in mortal sin!
Blessed are those whom Sister Death
will find in your most holy will,
for the second death
can do them no harm.
Praise and bless my Lord, thank him
and serve him humbly
but grandly!

And here, humbly but grandly, ends the story according to
Brother Leo: To the glory of God. Amen.

THE YEARS OF OUR LORD
1225–1226

Sister Death

And so he came to Siena. There they would try again to alleviate the pain and hemorrhaging of his eyes. There they failed again, and he began to feel a rapid deterioration in his whole body, and he knew that he must return to the Porziuncola where Sister Death was waiting to take him by the hand and lead him to where Jesus was waiting to take him by the hand and lead him to the Father.

The brothers who were with him, Angelo, Rufino, Leo, and Masseo, placed him upon a donkey, and so began the last journey to Assisi. He no longer wanted to be cared for by the brothers; he was ready to go home. Even riding on a donkey was hard. He could feel pain throughout his whole body, and every movement of the poor beast of burden was a burden to Francis. He no longer wanted to be borne along by any beast of burden. He was ready to go home, to fly from the Porziuncola with Sister Death, the angels flying beside them and before them, showing the way.

Most of the ride there he dozed or seemed to faint with pain as the donkey made its determined clopping way slowly toward the beautiful Umbrian valley from which he would enter Paradise. But just before descending from the Via Flaminia to the valley below where the Porziuncola waited patiently for his return, word came by messenger from Assisi that he was to stay first in the Bishop's palace so that the bishop's physicians could assess his health which Francis already knew was breaking down rapidly.

He would be obedient to his old friend, the Lord Bishop Guido, for his own will stood for nothing before the Church and her representative, the Bishop of Assisi. And so he came again to Assisi where a place had been prepared for him by the Bishop's household.

He lay there waiting for Jesus. But he wasn't there, his Lord and Savior. He was waiting for him at the Porziuncola, not here where Francis was born, not in Assisi, which he left when he renounced his father's patrimony. Assisi represented the world he left for the world of the Gospel that the brothers and the lepers inhabited at the Porziuncola. He loved Assisi because he was born there and because there he grew up and there he made his contract with the world of Assisi: that he would live a life of Gospel poverty, and they would witness his marriage to Lady Poverty.

But the world of Assisi had changed little in the values that it rejected and in the values of profit and power and violence that it embraced. And so he would bless this city he loved, but he would ask the brothers to take him to the Porziuncola where he could die in the arms of the Poor Christ.

As the brothers carried him on a stretcher down the hillside from Assisi, he had them stop so he could turn and bless the city. But just as he was beginning to bless, he saw the city transformed before him. Something had indeed changed. He saw all the brothers and Poor Ladies who came from there standing round the city like a ring of saints, and the people inside were kneeling and thanking God for all those who had left to serve the Poor Christ, and the people themselves seemed to him transformed; the world of the old Assisi was not winning but had been overcome by Christ. Then he heard the voice of the San Damiano crucifix saying, "I have overcome the world." And Francis, filled with thanksgiving and joy, raised his arms and blessed the city with words he had not anticipated saying but that the Spirit spoke through him:

> Lord, it is believed that in olden days this city was a refuge of evil people. But now it is clear that in your large mercy and at a time of your choosing, you have shown your special superabundant compassion. Through your goodness alone, you have chosen Assisi to be a place of refuge for those who know you in truth, who give glory to your holy name, and who waft toward all Christians the perfume of right reputation, holy life, true doctrine, and evangelical perfection. Therefore I pray you, O Lord Jesus Christ, father of mercies, not to dwell on our ingratitude, but remember always the immense compassion you have shown to this city. Let it always be a place of refuge for those who really know you and glorify your blessed name forever. Amen.[7]

Then he dropped his arms and bowed his head in shame that he had doubted God's love and mercy for his city, thinking that nothing had changed. He had been blind of heart, a thing worse than the blindness of his eyes. But God had shown him the wrongness of his judgment and in the words of the blessing had shown Francis how God himself viewed Assisi.

And the city wall itself began to shine like a crown of precious jewels enclosing the good people of Assisi. How good God is to have shown him the beauty of that which he thought was not beautiful, how God had made beautiful what Francis himself thought was ugly with the sins of greed and violence and petty hatreds.

Then there were the women like those women who stood by Jesus on his way of the cross, who stood beneath the cross, who, like Jesus's mother Mary and Mary Magdalene, kept alive the Good News of who he really was when he walked among them.

The two who came to Francis's mind immediately were the Lady Clare and Lady Jacopa dei Settesoli whom he affectionately called Brother Jacopa. Lady Clare, like his own mother Lady Pica, would not be there for him when he lay dying and yet would be more really there than some of those who would accompany his final days on earth. For we carry with us those who are the mirror of our own soul. And that is what the Lady Clare was. She mirrored the poor, crucified Jesus as no one else had, and Francis strove always to mirror this same Jesus, Francis and Clare then being mirrors of each other as each one was a mirror of the Christ they loved.

His own mother Lady Pica mirrored Mary, the Mother of Jesus, for him. For Mary, like his own mother, went looking for her Son in the temple when he was just a child, and when she and Joseph found him, had said, "Child, why have you treated us like this? See, your father and I have been searching for you in great anxiety." How many times his own mother had echoed words like those.

But Francis, unlike Jesus, did not go down to the Nazareth of Assisi with his mother and his father. He left, never to return. And Lady Pica bore it all in love. She would not be there for her son now, so important to a mother. How great must have been her own way of the cross during all those years without him—"Saint" Pica, his mother.

And Lady Jacopa, the Roman. She was even wealthier than his own father in money and property and heritage. On her father's side she was descended from the Norman knights who conquered Sicily, and her husband was of the great Roman family of the Frangipani whose castello stood on the boundary of the ancient Circus Maximus. She also had extensive properties in the area of Trastevere near the hospital of St. Blase where she made a small cell available to him when he was in Rome.

From their very first meeting Lady Jacopa understood and supported the brothers and their ministry. So deeply did she affirm the absolute poverty the brothers embraced that were her property her own and not her husband's, she would have left behind her riches and would have joined the lay

Franciscans whose numbers had grown large over the years. But what she could do and did was live detached from the riches she had because, like the brothers, she saw possessions as things lent to us by God out of which we are to generously share with those in need.

Sister, the Lady Clare, because of the enclosure of her life, would not be there at his passing which he knew would be the hardest of renunciations for her, the deepest poverty; but Brother, the Lady Jacopa, would come because she was free to do so. And he would ask her to bring with her the almond cookies she used to bake for him and the brothers when they were in Rome. How happy it will make her to be able to do something, especially to bake the cookies he delighted in when he was living in the cell at St. Blase's hospital. She will do for him what his own mother would have loved to do. May his dear mother rest in the arms of God.

They had arrived now at the other woman, the Porziuncola, the womb of the Order, Mary, Lady of the Angels. Here he had heard the Gospel that set the direction of the brothers' way of life. Here he had received the Lady Clare into the Order. Here he had received from Pope Honorius III, of happy memory, the pardon: a plenary indulgence for all punishment due to the sins of anyone who, having confessed their sins, came to Our Lady's small chapel he had repaired at her Son Jesus's injunction. Pope Honorius made this indulgence available each year on the day of the dedication of the Church of Our Lady of the Angels from the Vespers of the Vigil to the Vespers of the Feast of the Dedication.

. . . .

How sweet it will be to die here on the bare ground near his beloved Porziuncola. And yet...and yet nothing will be so sweet as to die in Jesus. Jesus in his heart and on his mind. Jesus on his lips and in his eyes and ears. Jesus in his hands and feet and side. Jesus everywhere.

Ever since the Angel of La Verna, he had been so immersed in Jesus that he saw clearly and with great consolation that this was Sister Death, this surrender to the suffering, dying Jesus. So much was yet to be done, so few converted, and only the disillusioned "Apostles and disciples" to carry on. This was Sister Death, this feeling of abandonment by the Father. This was Sister Death, this embrace of her who alone walks with us into eternity.

The consolation was the Spirit who would come to all those who kept trying to believe that what you said and did was of God. And so, as it was important for Jesus to say everything again as he did in his Discourse at the Last Supper with his Apostles, so Francis, too, would write his final word, his Testament. And the Holy Spirit would anoint his words at the Pentecost Chapter following his passing into heaven.

His words, like Jesus's words at the Last Supper, would say again who he was and who the brothers were and what manner of living would give them life and the sweetness of Jesus himself. The very core of what he wanted to say he would embed in two paragraphs, which, like the commandments Jesus gave us of love of God and neighbor, would contain all the other words. If these words alone were taken to heart and lived, then God's Spirit would illumine everything else he would say:

"This is how God inspired me, Brother Francis, to embark upon a life of penance. When I was in my sins, the sight of lepers nauseated me beyond measure; but then God himself led me into their company, and I worked mercy with them. When I had once become acquainted with them, what had previously nauseated me became sweetness of soul and body for me. After that I did not wait long before leaving the world....

"When God gave me some brothers, no one showed me what we were to do; but the Most High himself revealed to me that I was to live the life of the Gospel. I had this written down briefly and simply and His Holiness the Pope confirmed it for me. Those who embraced this life gave everything they had to the poor. They were satisfied with one habit patched inside and out, and a cord and trousers. We refused to have anything more."

That is all that the brothers needed to know. The rest of what he then wrote only clarified how Francis himself understood and lived their Rule approved by Pope Honorius. He asked that wherever and whenever the brothers read the Rule, they would read his Testament, too. It was his personal testament of what God had revealed to him. It was what Jesus showed him and what he had done. May the same Lord show the brothers what they were to do. May the Holy Spirit confirm and anoint the words of his Testament.

It was a matter of the heart and soul, he thought. No Rule could substitute for that. Either you heard the Gospel and responded to it as he and Bernard of Quintavalle had; or you did not. A Rule only reminded you of the promise you had already made to Jesus by doing what he counseled: "Take up your cross and follow me." The Rule only kept you true to the commitment you'd already made to the Gospel. The Rule was only a map of the life you were already living and a pledge that you would continue to do so. Without your own conversion and prior commitment to Jesus, the Rule was a curious document, an out-of-touch description of your founder's life, not your own.

Francis knew the commitment of the first brothers; he was not sure of the brothers who had come afterward and in such numbers. He hoped they didn't need the Rule but rather were grateful for it as a reminder of what Christ had already accomplished in them and where he had led them. "Come, Lord Jesus, lead us all into your footprints, the same footprints that led us on a journey with you when you called us by name, called us out of home and family to walk with you. No Rule will ever replace your call that Rules only transcribe and preserve for us."

. . . .

Now there was only the waiting, the hanging upon the cross with Jesus. "Lord Jesus, remember me, a poor sinner, when you come into your kingdom." And the waiting was hard as was the hanging there between this world and the next, between this intimacy of pain and suffering and the embrace of the Risen Lord, the two of them free of pain and with an eternity of that dialogue of love which is the gift of the Holy Trinity to those whose robes have been washed in the blood of the Lamb. He could not see to see what it would be like, but his heart knew that the heart of him he loved would be enough.

He asked the brothers to lay him naked upon the naked ground so that he could die like the naked Christ upon the cross. He asked them to leave him for as long as it takes to walk a mile. And so they did—until Brother Elias, the Minister General of the Order, intervened and commanded Francis under holy obedience that he be clothed in a borrowed habit and then be lifted from the ground onto his pallet.

How sweet this final poverty of not being allowed to die as he wanted and to be commanded under holy obedience to relinquish his own will to the will of his Minister, Brother Elias. Now he was ready. Now he had been stripped of his own will, even in death, a poverty more extreme than the stripping off of clothing that had begun his life in Christ. He had stripped himself of his father Pietro Bernardone's cloth as a sign that he was renouncing his patrimony in exchange for the patrimony of the kingdom of God. As a young man, he had stripped off his own clothes, but this stripping of his will by another was harder. He was willing the very stripping that was being done unto him. And so now he lay down upon a bed of his own choosing, though it had been foisted upon him by Brother Elias, the Minister of all the brothers.

And then he remembered once more the women beneath the cross of Jesus: His Mother Mary and his mother's sister Mary, the wife of Cleophas, and Mary Magdalene; and again Sister Clare and Brother Jacopa Settesoli came suddenly to mind. He asked for one of the brothers to hasten to Rome and summon the Lady Jacopa. "Tell her, dear brother, to bring with her some mostaccioli and whatever I will need for burial so that like Christ my body might be wrapped when it lies cold and abandoned by my living soul."

And behold, before the brother messenger could depart, there was the clamor of horse hooves outside, and into the place of the Porziuncola swept Lady Jacopa bearing the very gifts he had requested. The brothers tried to restrain her from entering the space where Francis now lay, but he gently reprimanded them saying, "Let *Brother* Jacopa enter, she who by her own covenant with God and us is indeed one of us."

And Brother Jacopa entered the sacred space of Sister Death bearing the mostaccioli (as the almond cookies he loved were called), a red silk cushion adorned with the family coat of arms, and her bridal veil embroidered with "*Ama, Ama, Ama*" (Love, Love, Love). Brother Jacopa then told how when she was praying in Rome, she had heard a voice which said that Brother Francis would shortly pass into heaven and that he would ask for the items which she in turn brought with her to Assisi.

Francis smiled and then, though weak and without any appetite but that of the spirit, he reluctantly ate of one of the mostaccioli and asked the brothers to join him in this final holy meal; for what is good in life is good in death, as well.

He then asked that the account of the Passion according to the Gospel of John be read to him. And when it had been prayerfully read, he intoned Psalm 141, and the brothers joined in singing it with him.

I call upon you, O LORD; come quickly to me;
    give ear to my voice when I call to you.
Let my prayer be counted as incense before you,
    and the lifting up of my hands as an evening
      sacrifice.

Set a guard over my mouth, O LORD;
    keep watch over the door of my lips.
Do not turn my heart to any evil,
    to busy myself with wicked deeds
in company with those who work iniquity;
    do not let me eat of their delicacies.
Let the righteous strike me;
    let the faithful correct me.
Never let the oil of the wicked anoint my head,
    for my prayer is continually against their wicked
      deeds.
When they are given over to those who shall
      condemn them,
    then they shall learn that my words were pleasant.
Like a rock that one breaks apart and shatters on
      the land,
    so shall their bones be strewn at the mouth of
      Sheol.

But my eyes are turned toward you, O GOD, my
      Lord;
    in you I seek refuge; do not leave me defenseless.
Keep me from the trap that they have laid for me,

and from the snares of evildoers.

Let the wicked fall into their own nets,

while I alone escape.

And thus did he escape into the embrace of Sister Death. He heard some of the brothers say that they heard the beat of bird wings and saw larks in the sky. What they could not see or hear was the Seraph-Man rising with Francis in his arms, an exaltation of larks fanning the air around them.

To the Glory of God. Amen.

AFTERWORD

Out of silence they came, words that helped me see Francis again. In this book I began to search for the Francis I found inside me years ago. I wasn't sure he'd still be there, but as soon as I began to hazard the first tentative words, I recognized the voice that spoke to me forty years ago when I was writing *Francis: The Journey and the Dream.*

I wondered at first if I was simply going over material that had been perhaps better articulated before; but try as I would to stop the emerging words, the voice would not stop but pressed hard upon my consciousness to record the words and to shape them into some kind of coherent narrative.

Eventually, this new story found its central motif in the words Gerard Manley Hopkins used to define St. Francis, namely, Christ's "Lovescape Crucified." It was this startling image that gave the story its controlling metaphor.

—*Murray Bodo, O.F.M.*
Feast of the Porziuncola
August 2, 2012

A CHRONOLOGY OF THE LIFE OF ST. FRANCIS

1182	Francis is born in Assisi; he is baptized John, but his father, returning from a trip to France, renames him Francesco ("Frenchman").
1193	Clare is born in Assisi to Favarone and Ortolana of the House of Offreduccio.
1198	The citizens of Assisi destroy the Rocca Maggiore, the fortress that towered above the city, a symbol of the Emperor's presence.
1199–1200	Civil war in Assisi results in the establishment of the commune.
1202 (November)	War between Assisi and Perugia. At the battle of Ponte San Giovanni, a town midway between the two warring towns, Francis is captured and taken as a prisoner of Perugia for one year.
1203–1204	Francis is freed and returns to Assisi. He is ill during the whole of the year 1204.
1205 (spring)	Francis decides to join the Papal Army in Apulia, south of Rome, which is under the command of Walter of Brienne. He leaves home and journeys only as far as neighboring Spoleto, where he is told in a dream to return to Assisi.

1205 (summer)

The final summer with his friends as "King of the Revels" in Assisi.

1205 (fall) The San Damiano Crucifix instructs Francis, "Go and repair my house which, as you see, is falling into ruin." Francis takes some of his father's cloth to Foligno and sells it. He gives the money to the priest of San Damiano, who refuses it, beginning of the final rift with his father.

1206 (spring)

Francis's father tries to take him before the civil court for the return of his money. When Francis says he is no longer subject to the civil authorities because he is consecrated to God, his father agrees to appear before Bishop Guido's tribunal. There Francis renounces his patrimony in front of the Bishop and assembled citizens and leaves for Gubbio, where he visits a friend and nurses lepers.

1206 (summer)

Francis returns to Assisi dressed as a hermit and begins to repair San Damiano.

1206 (summer)–1208 (February)

Francis repairs San Damiano, the small chapel of St. Peter (which is no longer standing), and the Porziuncola (St. Mary of the Angels).

1208 (February 24)

At the Porziuncola Francis hears the Gospel for the Feast of St. Matthias and embraces Gospel poverty. He changes his leather belt for a rope cincture. He begins to preach.

1208 (April 16)

Bernard of Quintavalle and Peter Catanii join Francis.

1208 (April 23)

Giles of Assisi joins them.

1208 (summer)

Three new members join.

1208 (late) The seven brothers go to Poggio Bustone and preach throughout the Rieti Valley. A new brother joins.

1209 (early) The eight return to the Porziuncola. Four more join them.

1209 (spring)

Francis writes a short Rule and leaves for Rome with his first eleven brothers. Pope Innocent III approves their way of life. They return and settle at Rivo Torto on the plain below Assisi.

1210 A peasant and his donkey invade their shed at Rivo Torto, and the brothers leave and go the Porziuncola, a short distance away.

1211 Francis plans to go to Syria, but high winds ruin his plans.

1212 (March 18–19)

Late in the night of Palm Sunday, Francis receives Clare into the Order at the Porziuncola and locates her first at the Benedictine Monastery of San Paolo delle Abbadesse in Bastia, and five days later Clare moves to Sant'Angelo in Panzo, the home of a group of penitent women. Several weeks later Bishop Guido provides the church of San Damiano as a monastery for Clare and her companions (including her sister Agnes, who has since joined them).

1215 (November)

Francis, in Rome for the Fourth Lateran Council, meets St. Dominic.

1216 (July 16)

Pope Innocent III dies in Perugia. Two days later Honorius III is chosen to replace him.

1216 (summer)

In Perugia, Francis obtains from Pope Honorius a plenary indulgence (sometimes called the Porziuncola Pardon) to commemorate the consecration of St. Mary of the Angels Church, which St. Francis called the Little Portion, the Porziuncola.

1217 (May 5)

At the General Chapter at the Porziuncola, the first missionary brothers are sent forth to cross the Alps and the Mediterranean.

1219 (late June)

Francis leaves Ancona for Acre in Syria, where he stays a few days before setting out, with Crusader reinforcements for the Fifth Crusade, for Damietta in Egypt where he will try to bring peace between the Crusaders and the Muslim forces.

1219 (fall) Francis meets and confers with the Sultan Malik al-Kamil, and the two become friends.

1220 Francis returns to Italy and resigns as minister general of the Order. He chooses Peter Catanii to replace him.

1221 (March 10)

> Peter Catanii dies. Brother Elias is designated vicar general.

1221 (May 30)

> A General Chapter. Francis writes his First Rule.

1223 At Fonte Colombo, Francis composes the Second Rule, to be discussed in the General Chapter in June. Pope Honorius III approves the Rule on November 29.

1223 (December 24–25)

> Christmas at Greccio in the Rieti Valley. Beginning of the live crèche and the spread of the custom of the Christmas crib throughout the world.

1224 (August 15–September 29)

> Francis goes to Mount La Verna in Tuscany to prepare for the Feast of St. Michael the Archangel, September 29. On September 14 or 15 he receives the sacred stigmata of Christ.

1224 (October and early November)

> Francis returns to the Porziuncola.

1224–1225 (December to February)

> Riding a donkey, Francis undertakes a preaching tour through Umbria and the Marches of Ancona.

1225 (March–May)

> His eyesight worsens; nearly blind, he spends some time at San Damiano, where he sings "The Canticle of the Creatures," sometimes called "The Canticle of Brother Sun."

1225   Francis adds a verse to "The Canticle" on pardon and peace, and a reconciliation takes place between the Bishop and mayor of Assisi when Francis sends one of the friars to the two men to sing "The Canticle" to them with the added stanza on pardon and peace.

1225   Francis is welcomed in Rieti by his friend, Cardinal Ugolino, the future Pope Gregory IX, who recommends his eyes be cauterized. Francis goes to the hermitage of Fonte Colombo for the cauterization.

1225 (September)

Another doctor tries to treat Francis's eyes.

1226 (April)

Francis is in Siena for another eye treatment.

1226 (May or June)

Francis is at Le Celle, a Franciscan hermitage in Cortona, where he dictates his Testament. He returns to the Porziuncola.

1226 (July and August)

Because of the heat, Francis stays at Bagnara, in the mountains near Nocera.

1226 (late August or early September)

His condition worsens, and he returns to Assisi, where he resides at the Bishop's palace.

1226 (September)

Francis senses his death is near and insists on returning to the Porziuncola.

1226 (Saturday, October 3)

Francis dies at the Porziuncola; he is buried the next day

in San Giorgio in Assisi, where today the Basilica of St. Clare has replaced the Church of San Giorgio.

1227 (March 19)

Cardinal Ugolino is elected Pope Gregory IX.

1228 (July 16)

Gregory IX canonizes Francis in Assisi.

1230 (May 25)

The body of St. Francis is transferred from San Giorgio to the new basilica constructed in his honor.

1253 (August 11)

St. Clare, the first Franciscan woman, dies at San Damiano and is buried in the Church of San Giorgio, where the body of Francis was first buried.

1255 (August 12)

Pope Alexander IV canonizes St. Clare at Anagni.

1259

Alexander IV ratifies by Papal Bull the move of the Poor Ladies from San Damiano to the Church of San Giorgio, where St. Clare's body lay buried. They were already residing there, having moved shortly after the death of St. Clare. They take with them to San Giorgio the crucifix that spoke to St. Francis at San Damiano, the silver and ivory pyx with which St. Clare had dispelled the Saracens, the iron grate through which they received Holy Communion and through which they had viewed the body of St. Francis for the last time. The Poor Ladies remain at San Giorgio, which is eventually replaced by the Basilica of St. Clare, where the Poor Ladies reside today.

NOTES

1. Murray Bodo, *Through the Year with Francis of Assisi* (Cincinnati: St. Anthony Messenger Press, 1993), p. 60.

2. Jacopone da Todi, *Laude* (Torino: Edizioni Pieme, 1999), p. 249. Author's translation. Original Italian available at http://www.gutenberg.org/files/29977/29977-h/29977-h.htm.

3. 1 Celano, 22, from Marion A. Habig, O.F.M., ed. *St. Francis of Assisi: Writings and Early Biographies: English Omnibus of the Sources for the Life of St. Francis* (Cincinnati: St. Anthony Messenger Press, 2008), pp. 246–247.

4. The Testament of St. Francis, from Bodo, p. 38.

5. Legend of Perugia, 43, from Habig, p. 1020.

6. Hopkins, Gerard Manley. *Poems.* Robert Bridges, ed. (London: Humphrey Milford, 1918), p. 43.

7. Mirror of Perfection, 124, from Habig, p. 1225.